MILLER POPE'S

Book of Pirates

ILLUSTRATED BY THE AUTHOR

Illustrations are created by the author, based on documentary sources.

Grateful acknowledgment is made to Cindy Vallar for permission to use her article "Pirate Lingo," which first appeared in her online newsletter *Pirates and Privateers*, as the basis for the chapter on "Pirate Lingo" in this book. Her site contains a great deal of detailed information: www.cindyvallar.com/bookaneer

Published by Winoca Press
P. O. Box 30
Wilmington, North Carolina 28402-0030
www.winocapress.com

Available from the publisher or your local bookseller, or from the author at www.millerpope.com

Printed in Canada
09 08 07   05 04 03 02 01

Library of Congress Cataloging-in-Publication Data

Pope, Miller.
    Miller Pope's book of pirates / illustrated by the author.
    p. cm.
    ISBN 978-0-9789736-2-9
    1. Pirates. I. Title. II. Title: Book of pirates.
    G535.P693 2007
    910.4´5—dc22

                                    2007024003

THIS BOOK WAS COMPOSED

in the Adobe Caslon, Adobe Jenson, and Lucida Blackletter fonts in Adobe InDesign CS2,
none of which were pirated

TO THE VICTIMS

✠

Contents

Acknowledgments

CREATING THIS BOOK HAS BEEN AN ADVENTURE in its own right. As a young boy I was fascinated by Robert Louis Stevenson's tales and Howard Pyle's rich illustrations of pirate lore. As an adult, I have traveled to shores throughout the world once frequented by pirates. But perhaps most of all I have enjoyed returning to the drawing board in retirement to envision what the pirates of yesteryear might have looked like, and to gather information about their ships, their weapons, their haunts, and their infamous exploits.

In preparing the book for publication, I would like to thank my colleague Ken Buckner, a talented photographer and designer; Jacqueline DeGroot, a novelist friend who has given me many good ideas; editor Betty Brannon, a doctoral student in folklore who checked my facts, grammar, and sentences; publishing consultant Nicki Leone, and editor and publisher Barbara Brannon. I would also like to thank my children, Debra and Gary, and my grandchildren for their patience and interest while I have been preoccupied with the project.

The information in this book was drawn largely from my lifelong love of history, from my years as a member of the Company of Military Historians, and from standard sources and popular websites, supplementing common knowledge and legend. General Web sources consulted include www.wikipedia.com, www.thepiratesrealm.com, www.candlelightstories.com/Pirates, and www.piratesinfo.com.

Illustrations are based on historical documents and portraits, where such exist, or from my own imagination. Many of the rogues depicted in the book borrow features from people I have seen in real life.

Although I practiced illustration in traditional media for more than six decades, when the personal computer made digital image manipulation feasible I adopted the technology early on. (Mac fans may be amused to know that I created my first digital art on a Lisa, the precursor to the Macintosh.) Today I paint most of my illustrations employing a digital pen and pressure-sensitive digital tablet in Corel Painter and Adobe Photoshop. Some of the graphics I created many years ago in pencil, pastel, or watercolor, for magazines that bought only first publication rights. Most are from my imagination or from digital photos taken the day before.

Technology is but one new tool in the illustrator's kit, however. The computer allows me to create more speedily and more easily what would have taken months in a former time—but the techniques and skills of illustration have been built on a lifetime of experience and learning. I hope that readers enjoy these depictions as greatly as I have enjoyed producing them.

MILLER POPE

Preface

PIRACY—THE ACT OF ROBBERY ON THE HIGH SEAS —is as old as civilization itself. Piracy was the scourge of the ancient Phoenicians, the Greeks, the Romans, and every other civilization that traded by sea. In some corners of the earth it remains a serious problem even today.

But it is sometimes difficult to define exactly who the pirates were, and who the victims. To the English, the explorer Francis Drake was a great naval hero—but to the Spanish and Latin Americans of his time he was a dreaded and notorious pirate. The people of Scandinavia are proud of their brave Viking heritage, yet to other Europeans of their time the Viking raiders would have been feared as nothing more than bloodthirsty pirates.

The line separating privateer from pirate was a thin one, and it was often crossed. A privateer was a sea captain legally authorized by one country to prey on the shipping of another, sometimes even when the countries involved were not officially at war. Such was the case when Queen Elizabeth I covertly authorized Drake and other English captains to plunder Spain's appropriated wealth as it was being transported from the New World and the Philippines.

In today's popular culture there is a tendency to regard pirates as romantic swashbucklers. The silver screen has abounded with Johnny Depp types swinging from the yardarms of tall ships flying the skull and crossbones, with cutlass in hand and a dagger clenched between their teeth. Real pirates were in fact nothing more than common criminals.

This book is not meant to be a scholarly history of pirates and piracy, although I have strived to make it as accurate as possible. It is rather the story of pirates at their peak of notoriety. Much of what is known about pirates of the "Golden Age" is based on stories passed down by other pirates—no doubt a highly embroidered version of the truth. But even if much pirate lore is fiction, enough fact remains to make a whale of a good story.

While the material in this book is based (as best I can discern) on accepted history, some aspects of pirate life will inevitably be disputed. For instance, I have included an illustration of "walking the plank." Many experts doubt that this punishment ever really occurred, but the legend is so ingrained in pirate lore that I did not want to omit it.

There are no existing portraits of most of the famous pirates—so I have taken the liberty to use my imagination. In this book Anne Bonny and Mary Read are depicted as beautiful women. Who knows; maybe in life they really were!

What constitutes the "Golden Age of Piracy"? Many would limit the period to the last decade of the seventeenth century and the first decades of the eighteenth century. To do so, however, would exclude some of the greatest and most influential pirates of earlier years, such as Sir Francis Drake and Sir Henry Morgan.

It is true that the height of piracy had come to an end by the mid-1700s. But to drop the curtain on the last act too soon would eliminate Jean Lafitte and others like him. Pirates have the same appeal to the modern imagination as the adrenaline-raising adventures of cowboy outlaws roaming the vastness of the American West. Just substitute the boundlessness of the seas for the plains and the desert and trade ships for horses— and you grasp something of the allure of pirates.

There is something in the human psyche that wants to put bygone bad guys on a pedestal. Jesse James, Billy the Kid, the Dalton Gang, and Butch Cassidy and the Sundance Kid from the Old West are just a few examples of the phenomenon. One only has to ask why Nazi uniforms sell to collectors for much more than British uniforms from the same war to realize this.

But even in their own time, pirates were often handsomely rewarded for their nefarious activities. Perhaps deep down, we admire their audacity and cunning. Piracy paid off well in more than riches for some. For instance, Drake was knighted, and Henry Morgan became lieutenant governor of Jamaica.

When most of us think of pirates we think of the pirates of the end of the sixteenth to the first part of the eighteenth century. Riches to plunder were pouring from the New World to the Old and from new colonies in Asia to the colonizing European homelands. The seas were vast, encompassing large unmapped or poorly charted regions where daring adventurers could hide. This was the golden age of piracy!

Miller Pope's Book of Pirates

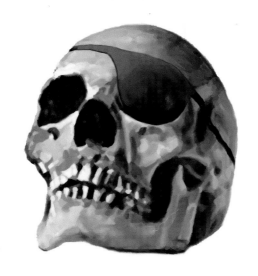

✝ PART THE FIRST

Race for Riches

THE QUEST FOR THE LOOT OF THE CONQUISTADORS BEGINS

New Discoveries and Spawn Piracy on the

In 1492, Christopher Columbus claimed the Caribbean island of Hispaniola—and the vast lands of the what would become the Americas—for Spain. The mother country was as eager for gold as for power in the New World.

New Riches Seven Seas

Europeans lusted for Indian gold.

IN THE FINAL DECADE OF THE FIFTEENTH CENTURY, two discoveries dramatically changed the Western world. The first was the arrival of Christopher Columbus to the New World in 1492; the second was Vasco da Gama's discovery of a sea route around Africa to the Orient in 1497.

Spain, which had commissioned Columbus's expedition, laid claim to all of the territory he discovered in the New World. In 1493 South America was divided between Portugal and Spain by Pope Alexander VI, and the race was on between the two powers to conquer territory in the Americas as well as to establish colonies and trading posts in the far East.

The flow of gold and silver from the New World steadily increased, becoming a flood as the conquistadors overtook native civilizations and claimed more of their lands. At the same time pearls, jewels, spices, silks, porcelain and other riches from their acquisitions in Asia flowed like a torrent across the Pacific and Indian Oceans. So convinced were the first Atlantic explorers

that in sailing west they had reached India and the Orient, they called the Caribbean islands the West Indies and the people they found there Indians—and so the mistaken terms remain today.

England, France, and the Netherlands yearned for a share of this wealth. For the next two centuries these nations would strive to gain a foothold in the West Indies in order to share in the vast riches found in the Americas. To obtain their objectives, they sometimes employed dubious means. In officially sanctioned wars, a privateering commission conferred by a letter of marque authorized a privately owned ship to attack the merchant vessels of a specified country and take a portion of the seized cargo as payment. In peacetime, a letter of reprisal was all the justification needed to attack the ships of a former enemy, ostensibly to recover any commercial losses incurred in an earlier war.

But officially sanctioned actions were hard to tell from outright piracy. Local merchants and government officials might legally invest in an ocean voyage, expecting their share of the profits in return for their risk. But where did the profits come from? Other ships and localities, of course. Such ventures might be fully legitimate in the eyes of their sponsors—while viewed by others as piracy.

If a corrupt government employee on an obscure island in the Caribbean were to grant a ship a commission to sail and then claim a share of the goods it captured, was the vessel a legitimate privateer or a pirate?

Was Sir Francis Drake legitimate when Queen Elizabeth I of England sanctioned his voyage and then took a share of the loot he brought home?

The profits to be made were large, and many weak central governments were prone to greed and corruption. The situation was very difficult to control. Actions protested as illegal by one group were often condoned by another.

The prospect of riches supplied ample inspiration for many sailors and adventurers to embark on a career of piracy without the bother or pretense of any form of official sanction.

Life on a merchant ship or in the navy was hard, and the pay was meager. Signing onto a voyage of months or even years brought the certainty of long, lonely stretches away from home and land, and the risk of illness, shipwreck, or worse. But life ashore for most was also harsh, with paltry rewards as well.

By contrast, the attractions of a life of free-ranging adventure with rich rewards beckoned many to the life of a sea-roving pirate. These enticements could be sufficient to outweigh the cruel deterrents of the sure

punishment if caught: dancing at the end of a rope and having one's corpse left to rot in a gibbet.

The piratical ranks were by no means filled only with desperate men or those of lowly means, however. The list included aristocrats, well-educated men, citizens of considerable wealth and status, and even one pirate who is believed to have written one of the great classic novels of English literature! And it included women as well.

A considerable number of pirates had little choice in their fate. They were perfectly honest seamen on ships that suffered the misfortune of capture by pirates. Given the unpleasant choice of joining the pirate crew or meeting their maker, many of them chose to avoid the meeting! However, once they joined with a pirate crew the authorities often made no distinction between the honest mariners and their pirate captors, and they could expect no mercy if captured.

But they were also treated as any other member of the crew, with the same rights and privileges as well as punishments. Every sailor, whether impressed into service or lured by the riches of the New World, stood to share in the bounty of plunder on the high seas. The lure was more than many could resist.

Sir Francis Drake commanded British ships that explored new lands and seized enemy property for the British crown.

Francis Drake, world explorer for England

The Dragon Singes King Philip's Beard

Sir Francis Drake was not the first sea raider to demand a share of the riches extracted from the new discoveries of Spain and Portugal—French pirates claimed that honor.

In 1522, Jean d'Ango of Dieppe captured Spanish caravels off the coast of the Azores carrying 45,000 gold pesos from Mexico. Soon other Frenchmen, like François le Clerc and Jacques de Sores, were raiding Spanish bases in the West Indies. De Sores held Havana for nearly three weeks in 1555 while he crammed his ships with gold and silver, slaughtered the inhabitants, and burned the settlement to the ground.

The Welsh-born privateer Francis Drake may not have been the first in these endeavors, but he was perhaps the most successful. His exploits as a raider of sea commerce and plunderer of Spanish riches are sufficiently extensive to merit his fame in the annals of pirates.

Drake's career on the bounding main began when he went off to sea at the tender age of ten, serving as apprentice and captain on small merchant vessels in the North Sea. In 1567, at twenty-three, he traveled to Guinea and the West Indies, this time as a ship's captain. His kinsman John Hawkins, who was in charge of a slave-trading expedition, had given him command of

Philip II, king of Spain

one of the flotilla's ships, the *Judith.* The expedition was attacked by the Spanish, and only Drake's ship, along with the *Minion,* captained by Hawkins, survived.

Young Drake proved the aptness of his name. "Drake" means dragon—and El Draco or El Draqui, as the Spanish called him, was breathing fire. He was eager for revenge and wanted to make up for the goods the

Spaniards had stolen from Hawkins's fleet.

Drake managed to procure a privateer's license from Queen Elizabeth I of England and set sail in his own ship in 1572. He devised a clever scheme to seize Spanish treasures from the Philippines by capturing the vulnerable port of Nombre de Dios on the Isthmus of Panama. Rich cargoes were transported across the Pacific by the Manila galleons, large oceangoing ships that were protected by armed escorts. Upon reaching Panama, however, they lacked a direct water route from the ocean to the Caribbean Sea, and were forced to unload goods and cross the narrow isthmus by mule train. At Nombre de Dios the treasure would be loaded again onto ships, to join the wealth of Spain's American colonies convoyed to the mother country.

Drake's initial plan to capture Nombre de Dios faltered when he was badly wounded in the attempt. But he was not resigned to failure. He remained in the area and the following year, joined by French buccaneer Guillaume le Testu, attacked the Spanish mule train as it crossed the isthmus. Their successful raid resulted in the capture of such a vast amount of silver and gold that the silver had to be left behind. From a height on the isthmus, Francis Drake also gained the distinction of becoming the first Englishman to gaze upon the Pacific Ocean.

Spain constructed massive harbor fortifications such as these at San Juan, Puerto Rico, in an attempt to deter Drake and other raiders.

Drake's plunder of the Isthmus of Panama allowed him to return to England a wealthy and famous man. But he was not content to rest on his laurels and enjoy his wealth. His spirit of adventure was not to be quelled. In 1577 he headed to the Spanish-owned Pacific coast of the New World. Traveling by way of the Straits of Magellan, he became the first Englishman to navigate that body of water.

Just before entering the straits Drake rechristened his ship, originally named the *Pelican*, as the *Golden Hind* in a gesture to his patron, Sir Christopher Hatton, whose coat of arms bore the image of a golden hind, or doe. His fleet was greeted by dangerous storms in the Pacific. One of his three ships, the *Marigold*, was destroyed and another, the *Elizabeth*, was so damaged that it had to be sent home. Drake continued north alone with only the *Golden Hind*.

After traveling up the Pacific coast of North America to what is today Washington state and finding no route across to the Atlantic, Drake turned back out into the Pacific. His sturdy ship took him to the islands of the Moluccas, the Celebes, and Java and westward around Africa's Cape of Good Hope. Drake once again returned to England laden with valuable treasure. He was also greeted with yet another first: he had been the first Englishman to circumnavigate the globe.

Francis Drake's great victories for England presented a problem for Queen Elizabeth. Acknowledgment of his successes would further alienate the Spanish, and the astute queen was reluctant to rouse the anger of Europe's most powerful empire.

Philip II, the powerful ruler of Spain, considered Elizabeth only the bastard daughter of an arch-heretic, Henry VIII of England. In the Escorial, a huge palace near Madrid that was almost as much a monastery as a palace, King Philip spent endless hours plotting Elizabeth's demise. His rage would be further stimulated by her bestowing honors upon the man who had stolen his treasure.

Coming to the realization that King Philip and the Spanish would never be placated, Queen Elizabeth paid Drake a visit aboard the *Golden Hind* and there conferred knighthood upon him.

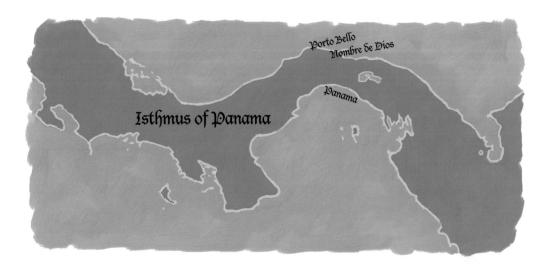

Drake's men plundered Spanish settlements in the New World.

The year 1585 found Sir Francis Drake once again at sea. He sacked and plundered Spanish cities in the West Indies and on the coast of Florida. On his homeward voyage, he visited Roanoke Island off the coast of North Carolina and picked up potatoes and tobacco—along with disillusioned colonists ready to return to England.

No aid could be spared for the little colony. In 1587 England was expecting the arrival of the largest invasion fleet ever launched—the Spanish Armada. This mighty host arrived the following year. The Dragon and the other English sea dogs, though outnumbered, confronted the great Spanish fleet in the English Channel. Superior tactics, gunnery, and seamanship overcame superior numbers, and the great armada was severely wounded and sent packing back to Spain. Only a pitiful remnant of the battered fleet were able to limp home.

Drake and Hawkins, with a fleet of twenty-seven ships, were sent to commandeer the riches of a damaged Spanish treasure ship harbored in Puerto Rico. But it had been more than five years since Drake's last encounter with the Spanish enemy, and he was unaware of how strong their defenses had become.

Drake lost the element of surprise when one of his smaller ships was captured. The Spanish were prepared for him at every port. As his remaining ships approached the coast of Puerto Rico two of Drake's officers were killed, and his own chair was shot from under him by Spanish guns. Drake survived, but the Spanish sank four ships, armed and loaded, to block his entrance to the harbor.

In Nombre de Dios and other ports people had been warned of his coming and their treasure had been hidden. Disappointed but still determined to find gold by other means, Drake set sail for Panama but fell ill with dysentery and died at sea off Portobelo soon thereafter. The fiery breath of the Dragon would sear Spain no more.

Francis Drake's estate, Buckland Abbey, in England

Drake's Golden Hind flew the colors of England (the red Cross of St. George) and bore the symbol of the deer.

The Buccaneers Discover Easy Money

THESE DAYS, WE OFTEN CONSIDER "BUCCANEER" as a synonym for pirate, but the name has an intriguing history of its own. In the early days, buccaneers plundered on both land and sea, while pirates limited their activities to the world's waterways.

On the Caribbean island of Hispaniola in the mid-seventeenth century, the *boucaniers* were a group of French hunters and traders known for their method of smoking meat on wooden frames called *boucans* to preserve it. The method itself was known as *barbicoa*—from which we also get "barbecue." When the Spanish killed off the wild game in hopes of forcing the French settlers off the island, the boucaniers soon turned to looting and plunder as a lucrative means of support.

Many of the boucaniers settled on the nearby small island of Tortuga, which today is part of Haiti. There they initially eked out a living by selling the preserved hides of wild cattle to Dutch traders. The Spaniards laid claim to Tortuga as well, but after they failed to drive the boucaniers away a second time, the island became a haven for pirates and fugitives from all nations. Many of the buccaneers who fled to Tortuga banded together in a society known as the Brethren of the Coast.

Islanders began to use the term buccaneer to describe all Caribbean pirates, and the English settlers in Jamaica soon picked up the custom. Within only a few years people everywhere knew what the name buccaneer meant: a wily, barbarous bandit roaming the tropical islands, showing no mercy, plundering at will.

By the 1640s the early buccaneers had set their sights squarely on the sea. They learned to sneak up astern of larger Spanish ships, usually under cover of darkness in small boats. Marksmen in the small rowboats held the Spanish helmsmen and soldiers at bay while other buccaneers swarmed up the opposite side of the ship.

The Caribbean buccaneers quickly earned a reputation of cruelty—especially against the Spanish who had driven them from their former homes—and were feared by all Spanish sailors.

Some buccaneers, like the notorious Nau the Olonese, acquired ships of their own and developed the speed and stealth to prevail against larger, more heavily armed Spanish vessels. They even sailed to the continent of North America, where they took to the practice of sacking towns.

The English, who had long sought to establish a viable presence in the Caribbean, were happy to enlist the aid of the buccaneers in harassing their Spanish rivals. In 1655, when the British at last drove the Spaniards from Jamaica, they rolled out the welcome mat for the buccaneers to base their ships at Port Royal in Jamaica

Bay. Many buccaneers moved to Port Royal, launching their raids from the port while the governor of Jamaica ignored or even encouraged them. Soon, the buccaneers were attacking entire towns on the Spanish Main, the Caribbean coast of the Spanish territories in Central and South America that served as a point of departure for New World riches being transported to Spain. The buccaneers greatly influenced the history of that part of the world, as their very presence on the high seas helped determine maritime trade routes. Hired to fight on the side of the British, they also won many battles in disputes over Caribbean territory.

Pirates were licensed as "privateers" by the British crown, which legalized their operations in exchange for a share of their profits. Britain sent buccaneers to attack French, Dutch, and Spanish shipping and colonies in

Tortuga

Hispaniola

the Caribbean. The vigorous trade, legal and illegal, soon made Port Royal the most prosperous city in the West Indies.

Britain even sent commissioned naval officers such as Christopher Myngs to lead the buccaneers, and their profitable activities continued in peacetime as well as in times of war.

Many buccaneers gained widespread notoriety because of their exploits. A Frenchman named Montbar was among the leaders of the buccaneers. His reputation for destroying Spanish ships and mercilessly killing as many Spaniards as possible earned him the name "the Exterminator." The most famous buccaneer was the Welsh privateer Henry Morgan, whose raids on Cuba, Venezuela, and Panama helped to ensure the survival of English interests in the Caribbean.

The buccaneers originated on the Caribbean island of Hispamiola.

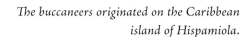

The buccaneers were at last put down by the French and English governments. In the early 1700s the interests of trade between the two countries triumphed, and the era of the buccaneers came to an end.

✠

Captain Henry Morgan,
privateer and royal governor

from Piracy
To a Governorship

THE EARLY LIFE OF HENRY MORGAN, whose name became nearly synonymous with the golden age of piracy in the Caribbean, is shrouded in uncertainty.

No one knows quite how Morgan came to leave his native Wales, where he was born about 1635. Some believe he joined troops under the command of England's General Robert Venables as a volunteer in 1654. Others claim he was kidnapped as a boy and sold as an indentured servant on the island of Barbados, where he then joined Venables's force. By the time Oliver Cromwell, Lord Protector of England and her Commonwealth, sent an army under Venables to attack the Spanish in the Caribbean in 1655, Morgan was on the scene.

The expedition failed, and the sorely defeated British army returned to its ships to plan the next move. Rather than return to England empty-handed, Venables's men sailed to the nearby island of Jamaica. In 1655 the beautiful island was a weakly guarded Spanish plum ripe for the picking, largely undeveloped, with only one major town. Venables took advantage of the opportunity and seized the island for the British crown.

But Venables had been expected instead to return to England with a more worthy Spanish prize, and his failure earned Cromwell's wrath. Both Gen. Venables and Vice-Admiral William Penn, commander of the fleet, were imprisoned in the Tower of London.

Among the ranks of British troops left to defend England's newest colony, tropical diseases and Spanish raids soon took their toll—though Morgan survived the hardships. The British governors turned to buccaneers, pirates, and other renegades to help guard the island. By the 1660s Port Royal had become a haven for thieves, murderers, pirates, prostitutes, and cheats.

During this lawless period Henry Morgan turned to a career as privateer. Early on he took part in the daring naval exploits and profitable raids on Spanish ports by British Vice-Admiral William Goodson and Commodore Christopher Myngs.

Morgan first captained a ship under Myngs during his 1662 raid on Santiago de Cuba. The attack was a major success—the town was captured and briefly occupied, and the infamous Castillo del Morro guarding the entrance to the Bay of Santiago was totally destroyed.

Morgan again sailed with Myngs as captain of a privateer ship during his daring 1663 move on San Francisco de Campeche, a Spanish stronghold. In another huge victory, the British captured fourteen Spanish ships and returned with vast amounts of rich plunder. Though Myngs soon returned to England, Morgan expanded his privateering endeavors. Attacks on Villahermosa, capital of the Mexican province of Tabasco, and the Nicaraguan silver mining center of Gran Granada proved very profitable for Morgan.

The raid on Gran Granada was especially risky for a seagoing privateer. Surrounded by dense, unexplored jungle, the large and prosperous city of Gran Granada was located on the shore of Lake Nicaragua, far from the coast. An attack on the inland city meant a swift, arduous, and undetected trek through the steaming jungle, but Morgan returned victorious, with rich spoils. His exploits earned him fame and respect among friends and foes alike.

Upon his return to Jamaica, Henry Morgan discovered that his uncle, Edward Morgan, had been appointed commander of all English troops in the West Indies. The younger Morgan's position was now secure. Following Edward Morgan's death, the governor of Jamaica appointed Henry commander of the militia in Port Royal. By 1668 Morgan was an English vice-admiral in command of a fifteen-ship fleet. Around the same time, the pirates elected Morgan to succeed Edward Mansfield as *their* admiral. In the dual role of English and pirate commander, Morgan became the scourge of all West Indian Spaniards.

Morgan undertook a series of raids on Spanish holdings—with the full commission and blessing of the governor of Jamaica, Sir Thomas Modyford. Morgan's first major attack, in 1668, met with trouble. He and

Sir Christopher Myngs

his crew were ambushed while trying to raid Puerto Principe, Cuba. The city fell to the privateers only after a bitter struggle and great loss of life. The rewards were few: the city's inhabitants had been warned of Morgan's coming and had hidden their treasure.

A ransom of fifty thousand pieces of eight—

paltry by pirate standards—paid for sparing the Spanish captives was all the return Morgan and his crew got for their efforts. Disappointed with their meager take, half of Morgan's crew quit. But Morgan was not discouraged. He announced a new plan for attacking Portobelo, Panama, a city richer than Puerto Principe but also more heavily fortified. Seasoned pirates scoffed at the idea. Morgan, however, had a strategy in mind.

Under cover of darkness Morgan and his crew slipped silently into the harbor of Portobelo in canoes. Though the city's first two forts fell quickly, the third repelled the pirate attacks. Morgan resorted to using Catholic priests and nuns to shield his crew as they climbed the walls of the fort. Portobelo surrendered to the attackers, and Morgan and his pirates made off with 250,000 pieces of eight and 300 slaves.

Word of the daring attack spread quickly, and Henry Morgan's force swelled to fifteen ships and nine hundred men. His ruthless tactics earned him the name "Morgan the Terrible."

Rumor of an imminent Spanish attack on Jamaica convinced Morgan and his buccaneers to launch a preemptive strike in October 1669. Morgan set sail this time for Cartagena, the most significant port along the

Spanish Main. In a stroke of bad luck his flagship, the *Oxford*, exploded when rum-soaked crew members lit candles too close to the ship's gunpowder stores, killing three hundred of his nine hundred men.

Reduced by a third of his strength, Morgan refocused his attentions on the harbor town of Maracaibo. But Morgan's ships were spotted. When the buccaneers arrived they found that the people had abandoned the town and taken their treasure with them.

Morgan took his fleet further into the Lagoon of Maracaibo, towards the town of Gibraltar. But again word had preceded him, and the population had fled. After eight unsuccessful weeks Morgan returned to Maracaibo. This time he was met at sea by Vice-Admiral Alonso del Campo y Espinosa, in command of three powerful Spanish warships.

The vice-admiral's imposing ship, the *Magdalen*, forty-eight guns strong, combined with the thirty-eight-gun *Santa Louisa* and the twenty-four-gun *Marquesa*, dwarfed the power of Morgan's own vessels, which typically had twenty guns or less each.

Battle ensued on May 1, 1669. Morgan ingeniously sent one of his ships, intentionally set ablaze and manned by a skeleton crew, in the direction of the *Mag-*

dalen. Once within range the fireship's crew lashed del Campo's ship to their own and lit fuses rigged to explosives before jumping overboard. The *Magdalen* burned and sank, the *Santa Louisa* ran aground as it fled, and the *Marquesa* was captured by the buccaneers.

Don Alonso managed to save himself by escaping into the fort of San Carlos Island, which guarded the mouth of the narrow Maracaibo Lagoon. Morgan may have held both the city of Maracaibo and all the ships—but Don Alonso controlled the only way out.

The Spanish citizens of Maracaibo agreed to pay a large ransom if the pirates would not burn the town. Morgan accepted. Don Alonso, however, stubbornly refused to pay the ransom or to let the pirates escape. A stalemate emerged between these bitter enemies. Meanwhile, from the heights of his fortress, Don Alonso watched as Morgan's men recovered the treasure that had sunk with his great Spanish warship.

With Spain's riches aboard, Morgan's only means of escape was still blocked. In a stroke of genius Morgan feigned a nighttime landing of his troops close to Don Alonso's fort. Obscured by moonlight, boat after boat of pirates appeared to land on the beach. In truth, the boats carried the same crew members each time! As the pirate longboats rowed landward the crew sat upright, but during each return of the apparently empty boats they lay flat, out of sight.

By daybreak Don Alonso was convinced that several hundred pirates were planning a land-based attack and ordered all of his guns moved to the landward side of the fort. Morgan's ruse had succeeded. From the deck of his new flagship, the *Marquesa*, Morgan ordered his crew to set sail with the tide, slipping unchallenged through the mouth of the unguarded channel.

Morgan returned to Port Royal in triumph with a treasure of 250,000 pieces of eight and a reputation for skill and cunning leadership. With his newfound wealth, he devoted the following year to the growth of his sugar cane plantations, focusing on his status as a prosperous land owner rather than his infamy as a privateer. His Spanish foes welcomed the break.

But Morgan did not stay idle for long. Under a new commission in 1670 to capture the great Spanish treasure in Panama, he united the two main pirate forces of the Caribbean, those from Port Royal and those from Tortuga. Morgan set sail with thirty-six captains and 1,800 men. Morgan's men followed in the footsteps of Sir Francis Drake the previous century, through the dense jungles and mountains of the Isthmus of Panama.

In a success that had eluded Drake, Morgan's forces

Morgan commanded a force of 1,800 men.

survived the journey across the isthmus. Arriving at the city of Panama, they confronted Spanish soldiers under the command of Gov. Guzman, viceroy of Panama, on January 19, 1671. Morgan's troops were outnumbered, but his fearsome reputation had spread, and the demoralized Spanish resistance quickly crumbled. The city fell and was burned to the ground. Some believe that Morgan also ordered the slaughter of all remaining Spanish inhabitants of the city.

Although Morgan's men had seized 400,000 pieces of eight from the sacked Spanish city, they were disappointed: from one of the richest cities in the world they had expected more. News of Morgan's coming had reached Panama, and the merchants had spirited away sizable fortunes along with silver from Peruvian mines.

To make matters worse, when Morgan and his men returned to their ships on the north side of the isthmus in March 1671, he learned that their attack on the Spanish city had violated a peace treaty signed between England and Spain shortly after his departure from Port Royal. Spain was on the verge of declaring war on England because of the breach of the peace treaty.

Gov. Modyford was arrested and sent back to England to be imprisoned in the Tower of London, but this did little to placate Spain. As more news of Morgan's excesses and atrocities reached Europe, Spanish protest increased, and in 1672 Spain called for Morgan's arrest. The new governor, Sir Thomas Lynch, was at first reluctant to carry out the order, fearing the pirates' reprisal, but in April 1672 sent Morgan to England as a prisoner of the country who had, for almost twenty years, sanc-

tioned the very actions for which he was now charged.

When war subsequently erupted between Holland and England, Gov. Lynch found himself in a difficult position. Jamaica's lucrative sugar trade was threatened, and the buccaneers could do little without their leader. What was to be done?

Instead of punishing Morgan, England's King Charles II sought his advice on the situation. Soon Henry Morgan was his way home again to Jamaica as

King Charles II of England conferred knighthood on Captain Henry Morgan.

lieutenant governor under Lord Vaughan, who would succeed the luckless Gov. Lynch. And to top it all off, the infamous Welsh privateer had been knighted by the king. He returned to Port Royal as Sir Henry Morgan!

Morgan's pirating days were over. Upon his return to Jamaica he settled down to life as lieutenant governor in the island's council and became a respectable man of power and status. He spent most his remaining years overseeing the island's defenses and expanding his fortunes as a sugar planter. In a bit of irony, one of Morgan's duties as lieutenant governor was to rid the seas of all buccaneers—a job he must have done well since, at the time of his death on August 25, 1688, there were very few left.

Sir Henry Morgan, the Pirate King, was the most feared and most respected buccaneer of all time. He had certainly been ruthless in the execution of his bloody trade, and he had no doubt been brutal at times, though he had never been the sadistic, drunken lout some tales made him out to be.

Morgan contributed tirelessly to the building of Jamaica. But all traces of his work were obliterated shortly after his death: on June 7, 1692, a massive earthquake hit the island colony, destroying Port Royal and Morgan's grave along with it. The city he had done so much to build was wiped off the map.

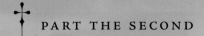 PART THE SECOND

Greed & Gold

THE PRACTITIONERS
OF PIRACY
AND THEIR METHODS

Taking a Ship

Pirates aspired to overtake the wealthy merchant ships they had targeted with as little damage to ship and booty—the captured treasure—as possible. They often needed only to fire a warning cannon shot, or a precise hit to break the mainmast or bowsprit, to guarantee a quick surrender.

If the pirates needed to get in closer they would attempt to cripple the merchant ship by bringing down sails, lobbing grenades, or picking off select victims with musket shots.

But pirates generally commanded lightly armored ships that, though small and swift, could seldom rely on firepower alone. The speed and maneuverability of their vessels allowed them to quickly overtake their prey or elude pursuit, but they were vulnerable to more heavily armed vessels.

Instead, the pirate ship would draw alongside the merchant vessel. The crew would throw grappling hooks over the side to lash the merchant vessel to their own. With their victims unable to flee, the pirates would swarm aboard the unfortunate ship, weapons drawn and ready for a fight on deck. Though often outnumbered, the pirates usually met with little resistance from frightened merchant crews.

The greedy pirates would completely loot the captured ship, taking everything they wanted. They typically plundered weapons, medicine chests, flags, tools, ropes, and sails. Seized weapons were especially prized by the victors. But the greatest spoils came from the lucrative cargo carried by the captive ships. Pirates could turn a handsome profit from the sale of stolen gold, silver, jewels, sugar, tobacco, and spices.

As a final blow, the pirates often laid claim to the entire ship, even forcing the hapless captive crew to join them in further escapades.

Life and Work aboard a Pirate Ship

DURING THE PEAK YEARS OF PIRACY in the Caribbean, pirates simply converted cargo vessels—often captured merchant ships—for use as pirate raiders. Captured ships were rarely outfitted for the rigors of the pirate trade. However, extra armament and a large crew was often all that was needed to turn an ordinary cargo carrier into an acceptable pirate ship.

Smaller vessels with shallow drafts often made the best pirate ships. They were fast enough to overtake the pirates' intended victims yet highly maneuverable, allowing for a quick and effective escape if needed. Pirates most often preferred the schooner, the sloop, and the brigantine.

The sloop was the most common pirate ship used in the Caribbean during the seventeenth and eighteenth centuries. Like its American cousin the schooner, the sloop could carry up to seventy-five men and fourteen guns, and could weigh as much as 100 tons. Its single mast and large spread of sail made the sloop fast, capable of making up to eleven knots, as well as agile.

The brigantine was a larger ship prized among pirates sailing in American coastal waters. A two-masted ship capable of carrying as many as 100 men and a dozen small cannon, a brigantine measured up to eighty feet long and weighed up to 150 tons.

A brigantine's foremast was fitted with square-rigged sails, while the mainmast carried a fore-and-aft-rigged mainsail and square-rigged topsail. This combination allowed for the greatest speed in varying wind conditions, and the ship's shallow draft permitted excellent maneuverability in often treacherous coastal waters.

While the slighter, swifter sloop and schooner were invaluable in quick attacks, the larger, more heavily armed brigantine was well suited for prolonged battle.

Pirate ships, particularly larger vessels, were often constructed of cedar and oak, making them both sturdy and buoyant. Their sails were made of tough canvas woven from hemp, cotton or linen, and the ships' riggings were made of tightly woven hemp lines that supported the weight of the mast and sails. Wooden yardarms secured the sails to the masts; crew members could climb woven ratlines to take in or let out the sails according to weather conditions. When not in use, a ships' sails were stored in the driest area below decks to prevent rot.

A ship's surface was separated into decks. The raised deck near the bow (the front of the ship) was called the forecastle or f'o'c'sle, while the higher deck at the stern (the rear) was named the sterncastle. Above the sterncastle was the quarterdeck, where the helm, or ship's wheel, was located. The captain's and officer's quarters were located just under the quarterdeck.

The gun deck housed the ship's cannons just beneath the main deck. In such confined quarters there was always the risk of fire or explosion. Gunpowder was thus stored in a magazine usually located on a lower deck near the stern, well away from the stove in the ship's galley. Smoking was banned below decks.

Large barrels filled with fresh water were placed down in the ship's hold to act as ballast, stabilizing the vessel against the roll and pitch of the ocean.

Ships were steered by massive wooden rudders linked to the ship's wheel. Winches called capstans controlled the anchors, which could weigh up to 3,000 pounds. Often it required the strength of five or six crew members to raise and lower the anchors.

Living conditions aboard a pirate ship could be harsh. The crew's quarters were cramped, smelly and dirty, and fresh food and water were often scarce. The stored barrels of ballast water provided the crew's only supply of drinking water. To conserve resources, rum or grog (rum mixed with warm water and lemon) were more commonly drunk.

Meat that was salted down and packed in barrels below deck often rotted. What the crew didn't eat, the ever-present rats were happy to consume. Sailors sometimes fished or went ashore to hunt, if they lacked preserved meat, they could always rely on hardtack, a dry cracker-like wafer made of little more than flour and water. Hardtack kept for months and could be soaked in coffee, brine, or any other liquid to create an adequate, if less than tasty, pirate meal.

Barque or bark. The term for small vessels before the 1700s; later applied to a small three-masted ship. This fast ship with shallow draft was a pirate favorite.

Barquentine or barkentine. A sailing ship of three or more masts, square-rigged on the foremast and fore-and-aft rigged in the remaining masts.

Brig. A two-masted sailing ship, square-rigged on both masts.

Brig

Brigantine. Originally a small Mediterranean ship with both sails and oars. It got its name from pirates: *brigantino* meant "brigand's ship" in Italian. Later the name referred to a two-masted sailing ship with its fore-mast square-rigged and fore-and-aft sails on its main mast. Eventually the word was divided into *brig* and *brigantine*, each word referring to different classes of ships. A brig was a re-rigged, more powerful ship.

Brigantine

Caravel. Originally a small lateen-rigged ship, around 80 feet long, meant for trading that later developed into the square-masted ship used by the Spanish and Portuguese for exploration.

Carrack. The largest ship before the galleon, the Spanish and Portuguese used the carrack for trading voyages to the Orient and the Americas. It had three masts with square sails on the fore and main masts and lateen sails on the mizzen. Such a powerful ship could only be taken by stealth.

Dhow. This 150- to 200-ton trading ship had a single lateen-rigged mast. Arab pirates armed their dhows with cannon.

Frigate. This term may have come from the Latin word *fabricata*, meaning something built; possibly adopted from the name of a ship which may have carried oars. Around 1700, the English used the word to describe a class of warship second in size to the ship of the line (battleship). This three-masted ship with anywhere from 24 to 38 guns was sometimes used to hunt pirates. Very few of these powerful ships came into pirate use.

Frigate

Fuste or fusta. A small fast ship with both sail and oars, favored by Barbary corsairs, who operated in the Miediterranean Sea.

Galiot. A long, sleek, oar-powered ship with a flush deck with two to ten small cannon. The galiot carried as many as 130 men and was used by Barbary corsairs.

Galleon. A large, slow cargo ship, the primary vessel of the Spanish treasure fleets. Galleons were unable to sail into or near the wind, and their heavy cannon defended against direct assault. Most had two to three decks and three masts.

Galley. A mainly oar-powered ship of ancient origin, sometimes used by the Barbary corsairs in the

Mediterranean. Captain Kidd used a version with both oar and sail, rigged like a frigate, the *Adventure Galley*.

Junk. A flat-bottomed ship with no keel, a flat bow, and a high stern. Junks were very seaworthy, with two or three masts with square sails made from bamboo, rattan, or grass. The word derives from *djong*, the Javanese word for ship.

Ketch. A ship with two masts fore-and-aft-rigged. The mizzenmast of a ketch is stepped aft of a taller mainmast but forward of its rudder.

Longboat. A very long rowboat carried on ships; used for coming and going to the ship. Often a longboat possessed a removable mast and sail.

Man-o'-War or Ship of the Line. The largest warship of the day, often armed with more than 100 guns. Only the major sea powers possessed these powerful 1,000-ton giants. Theses battleships had three masts, which were square-rigged, except for a lateen sail on her aft mast.

Man-o'-War

Merchant or Pink. From the Italian word *pinco*, the term pink was used mostly in the Mediterranean to describe a small, flat-bottomed cargo ship with a narrow stern. The Dutch word *pincke* was used in the Atlantic to describe small a ship with a narrow stern, usually square-rigged.

Schooner. A narrow-hulled, two-masted ship of under 100 tons, usually rigged with two large sails suspended from spars reaching from the top of the mast toward the stern. Other sails sometimes were added. The schooner's shallow draft enabled it to await prey in

shallow coves. The schooner was favored for its speed and space for a large crew.

Schooner

Shebec. The shebec, large and fast with both sails and oars and carrying up to twetny-four cannons, was a favorite of Barbary pirates. It could carry as many as 200 crew. The shebec had three masts, which were usually lateen-rigged, and a pronounced overhanging bow and stern.

Shebec

Sloop. A fast, agile shallow-draft ship of as many as 100 tons, used mainly in the Caribbean and Atlantic. Sloops were generally rigged with a large mainsail that was attached to a spar above, to the mast on its foremost edge, and to a long boom below. They often had additional sails, both square- and lateen-rigged.

Tartan. A fast, manueverable, and narrow Arabic ship used in the Mediterranean by the Barbary pirates. The Tartan carried one mast with a lateen mainsail and a small foresail on the bowsprit. It also had around thirty oars, fifteen per side. A small mizzenmast with a lateen sail was sometimes added.

Laws of the Lawless

STRANGE AS IT MAY SEEM, pirate crews traditionally operated as a democracy. Captains were elected by the crew and could be replaced by a vote of the crew. The captain had to be a leader and was expected to fight alongside his men in combat rather than lead them from a distance. He also had to know how to handle and navigate a ship. In practice this narrowed any competition for the captain's job.

Pirate captains were elected by the crew from among themselves.

Once elected, the captain walked a precarious path. During raids he maintained absolute authority, but at other times he was subject to the scrutiny of his crew. If he failed to participate in battle or failed to attack a desired ship, the crew could mutiny. They could either vote him out of his envied position or worse, maroon him. Many a pirate ship changed hands this way.

Pirates also maintained a sort of social insurance

system. Injured pirates were compensated for their losses. A maimed pirate might receive 100 pieces of eight for the loss of an eye or a finger, or 500 pieces of eight for the loss of a left arm or right leg.

When the pirates successfully captured a ship, the spoils were divided among the crew. Officers were awarded a greater share because they took greater risks or had special skills, but the entire crew shared equitably in the plunder.

Of course, pirates were not always totally democratic. The crews of captured ships were not generally given a realistic choice about joining the pirate crew. Specialists such as carpenters were valuable to the pirates and were sometimes forced to serve with them for extended lengths of time. However, they were usually released when no their services were longer needed.

Most pirate crews agreed upon written rules of conduct, or charters, in order to prevent disputes. The following often-quoted charter was drawn up by the crew of Capt. Bartholomew Roberts (see more about "Black Bart" on pages 82–85).

1. Every man shall have an equal vote in affairs of moment. He shall have an equal title to the fresh provisions or strong liquors at any time seized, and shall use them at pleasure unless a scarcity makes it necessary for the common good that a retrenchment may be voted.

2. Every man shall be called fairly in turn by the list on board of prizes, because over and above their proper share, they are allowed a shift of clothes. But if they defraud the company to the value of even one dollar in plate, jewels or money, they shall be marooned. If any man rob another he shall have his nose and ears slit, and be put ashore where he shall be sure to encounter hardships.

3. None shall game for money, either with dice or cards.

4. The lights and candles shall be put out at eight at night, and if any of the crew desire to drink after that hour they shall sit upon the open deck without lights.

5. Each man shall keep his piece, cutlass, and pistols at all times clean and ready for action.

6. No boy or woman to be allowed amongst them. If any man shall be found seducing one of the latter sex and carrying her to sea in disguise, he shall suffer death.

7. He that shall desert the ship or his quarters in time of battle shall be punished by death or marooning.

8. None shall strike another aboard the ship, but every man's quarrel shall be ended on shore by sword or pistol in this manner: at the word of command from the Quartermaster, each man being previously placed back to back,

shall turn and fire immediately. If any man do not, the Quartermaster shall knock the piece out of his hand. If both miss their aim, they shall take to their cutlasses, and he that draws first blood shall be declared the victor.

9. No man shall talk of breaking up their way of living till each has a share of a thousand pounds. Every man who shall become a cripple or lose a limb in the service shall have eight hundred pieces of eight from the common stock, and for lesser hurts proportionately.

10. The Captain and the Quartermaster shall each receive two shares of a prize, the Master Gunner and Boatswain, one and one quarter, and private gentlemen of fortune one share each.

11. The musicians shall have rest on the Sabbath Day only, by right, on all other days, by favor only.

Punishment at Sea

WALKING THE PLANK IS perhaps the most widely depicted form of piratical execution, but it will surprise many to learn that it rarely, if ever, happened. In the popular media the image of the hapless victim being forced, hands bound, to jump from a wooden plank or beam extended over the side of a ship into shark-infested waters, is common. In reality most pirates preferred the less dramatic practice of simply throwing victims overboard.

The cat-o'-nine-tails was an instrument of severe physical punishment. It was commonly used aboard British naval vessels, and by some pirates, for flogging, or whipping, those who failed to follow the code of conduct.

"The cat" likely got its name from the strands that left lashes on a sailor's back like bloody scratches from a cat's claws. The nine "tails" of the whip were traditionally made from braided strands of rope or leather, each bearing a knot near the bottom. Below the knot, the strands remained unraveled to inflict maximum punishment. Any pirate unfortunate enough to be flogged could also expect to have his open wounds doused with buckets of salty sea water.

Keelhauling comes from the Dutch *kielhalen*, which means "to drag along the keel." While some Western pirates adopted this form of punishment, it is more prevalent in pirate lore than it was in actual practice. The guilty sailor was tied to a rope that looped beneath the vessel and thrown overboard on one side of the ship. The sailor was then dragged under the ship's keel before being pulled from the water on the other side. Between the shock of the icy-cold ocean waters, the danger of drowning, and the injuries and infections caused by razor-sharp barnacles on the bottom of the ship, keelhauling a particularly brutal form of punishment. It is no wonder pirates adhered so closely to the code.

Marooned!

AROONING, THE PRACTICE OF intentionally leaving someone behind in an uninhabited area, was a pirate's most dreaded punishment. It was a cruel fate reserved for those who committed the most serious infractions such as stealing from another crew member, murder, or abandoning one's post in battle. It was also the fate of many an unfortunate captain in the case of mutiny.

The doomed pirate would be left on a deserted island—where *maroons*, or escaped black slaves, had once fled—often with only a day's worth of fresh water and a loaded pistol. He was then faced with the agonizing choice of a slow, painful death from a lack of food, water and shelter or taking his own life, which would condemn his immortal soul.

Some pirates became pirate hunters.

The Hunters Were Also the Hunted

Piracy was a high-risk occupation, with the noose and gibbet always looming. Merchants and governments offered attractive incentives for the capture of pirates, and bounty hunters set out to claim these handsome rewards.

The ranks of pirate hunters included noblemen and naval officers—and often former pirates who had been pardoned and sought a new way to earn a living. At least one well-known pirate, Capt. Kidd, started out as a pirate hunter and became a pirate instead!

Among the first of the great pirate hunters was a Spanish nobleman, Pedro Menéndez de Avilés, who wiped out the French settlement in Florida and destroyed the Huguenot pirates under orders of the Spanish king in the 1500s. Later military heroes will forever be linked to the infamous pirates they brought to surrender: Lieutenant Robert Maynard, who chased down and killed Blackbeard; Colonel William Rhett, who captured Stede Bonnet; and Captain Challoner Ogle, who killed Black Bart Roberts.

Woodes Rogers, once a pirate himself, became the governor of New Providence and dispatched pardoned pirates to round up the unpardoned. Ex-pirate Benjamin Hornigold turned and pursued pirates Stede Bonnet and Charles Vane, among others. Pity the pirate who didn't know which side his former conspirators fought for!

Pirates Didn't Always Win

JOHN DANIELL, A SOUTH CAROLINA ship owner in colonial times, once devised a shrewd way of evading capture by pirates—as the story goes.

Daniell was engaged in shipping between London and the busy port of Charleston, where pirate ships often lurked just over the horizon with an eye for homebound prey.

On just such an occasion in 1717 as Daniell's ship neared Charleston, a pirate vessel was spotted in the distance. Daniell calculated that the pirate ship, having the wind, would overtake his ship before he could reach safety. He arrived at a clever but desperate plan. He issued two orders that must have struck the crew as bizarre: he told them all to put their shoes on, though they customarily often went barefoot, especially in warm weather. He then ordered them to quickly gather everything made of glass on his ship and smash it. The shards of glass were then spread all over the deck.

When the barefooted pirates overtook the vessel and came swinging aboard they were greeted by a most unpleasant experience. They found themselves at such a disadvantage that they were overcome by the well-shod crewmen of the merchant ship, and their own ill-gotten treasury came into the possession of Daniell and his crew. The pirates' misfortune became the fortune that enabled John Daniell to purchase a fine plantation on the coast of North Carolina, living out his days there safe from further incidents with pirates.

✠

Buried Treasure

NOTHING MORE ENTICING OCCURS in pirate literature and folklore than images of sea chests overflowing with pieces of eight, plundered gold, and exotic gems—buried on island beaches and hidden in remote caves. But documented examples of pirates who buried their plunder are rare. With the possible exception of Captain Kidd, tales of buried treasure are almost certainly romanticized works of pirate fiction.

Pirate ships were not as a rule heavily fortified, and most Western pirates confined their attacks to lightly armed merchant ships. Merchant cargo generally consisted of silk or cotton, slaves, barrels of rum or tobacco, medical supplies, tools, weapons, food, and a few coins (in the Spanish world, pieces of eight). A rare ship- ment might include more valuable stores such as spices, indigo, or sugar.

A few especially daring pirates did acquire enormous wealth during piracy's golden age by preying on the vast riches of the Spanish Main. However, life at sea was hard, and the very nature of piracy made for an uncertain future at best, so most pirates preferred to spend their ill gotten gains on drinking, gambling, and women when they returned to port.

Without a doubt more money has been spent on searching for the pirates' elusive treasures than the pirates themselves ever actually buried.

Oak Island

The Money Pit ●

The Real Treasure Island?

ROBERT LOUIS STEVENSON's great pirate novel *Treasure Island* is a work of fiction. But there is a real island only four miles off the coast of Nova Scotia, Canada, that almost certainly contains a great treasure.

In 1795, a sixteen-year-old boy exploring Oak Island noticed a circular depression in the ground and with the help of two friends began to dig. After they had uncovered one layer of logs and one layer of stone, the boys gave up. Nine years passed before they persuaded others to help them resume digging.

After having reached a depth of 98 feet after many days of arduous work, they returned one morning to find the shaft they had dug full of water. No exertion was sufficient to pump out the water. To this day despite the expenditure of vast sums of money and human sweat and the cost of human lives, the water remains.

At the eastern end of the island a natural shaft or blowhole apparently once led downward some 200 feet below the surface. Some brilliant mind designed a way to block the shaft with a series of platforms and partially flood it through side tunnels. The "money pit" cannot be accessed without flooding the shaft entirely with seawater unless the tunnels deep in the ground can be dammed first.

In 1970 a salvage company using modern equipment reached a depth of 212 feet and discovered the cave at the base of the shaft. Underwater cameras revealed old logs on the cave floor and, it was said, three chests and a human hand severed at the wrist.

Someone went to a great deal of trouble to hide something of great value on the little island. Oak Island just happens to closely resemble an island on a treasure map—believed by many to be authentic and attributed to Captain Kidd (see more about him, pages 68–72).

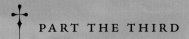 PART THE THIRD

Tools of the Trade

THE INSTRUMENTS
AND IMPLEMENTS
OF PIRATICAL PLUNDER

Shipboard cannon

Pirate Weapons and Gear

PIRATES DEPENDED ON READY ACCESS to a wide array of powerful weaponry to ply their perilous trade. The type of weapon a pirate crew used often depended on when—or if—their prey surrendered. But the aggressors had to be prepared for any situation. Cannons were effective in disabling ships from a distance, while muskets and grenades inflicted further damage at closer range. If their victims resisted, or if a determined pirate hunter came aboard hoping to claim the bounty placed on a pirate's head, knives and pistols were essential in hand-to-hand combat.

Pirates were willing to risk death in pursuit of their ill-gotten gains, but they knew they could not enjoy the fruits of their plunder if they wound up in Davy Jones's Locker—deep beneath the waves at the bottom of the cold, dark sea.

MEDIUM- TO LONG-RANGE WEAPONS.

Cannons and artillery. Ships' cannons were categorized by the weight of the shot they fired, and ranged in size from small two-pounders to impressive forty-two-pounders. Each cannon required at least four men to load, fire, and aim. By the eighteenth century cast-iron cannons had become considerably more accurate in range and speed than earlier bronze cannons. At a distance of 700 to 1,000 yards, a standard cast-iron ball could take down a ship's masts and rigging, sending deadly splinters flying along its deck. Other types of shot were designed to disable a ship at a range of only 50 to 500 yards.

Bombs and shells. Hollow cast-iron balls filled with gunpowder. Each shot was topped with a length of fuse timed to explode on impact. A bomb's range was almost the same as that of a standard cannonball, but it did more damage upon arrival.

Bar shot. Two small iron cannonballs or two halves of a shot attached by iron bars. Bar shot was capable of taking down sections of mast, putting holes in a ship's deck, or ripping sails to shreds. The shot's erratic trajectory could not be controlled, so it was used at a shorter range than the bomb or other forms of cannon shot.

Chain or knipple shot. Two small iron balls joined by a length of chain. Knipple shot was similar to bar shot but was most widely used at medium range to destroy sails and rigging, preventing a targeted ship from maneuvering or fleeing.

Heated or hot shot. A solid iron cannonball heated to a red-hot state and used to set flammable targets ablaze. Hot shot was an effective tactic in the days of wooden ships, but it could also be a hazard for crew members tending the cannon. If not loaded and fired properly, the superheated shot could cause the cannon's gunpowder to explode prematurely.

CLOSE- TO MEDIUM-RANGE WEAPONS.

Stinkpots. Small clay pots usually filled with burning sulfur and other noxious compounds. Stinkpots were lobbed onto the deck of a ship, emitting thick

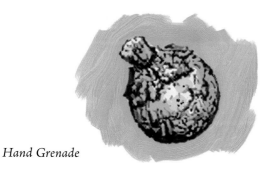

Hand Grenade

Bomb

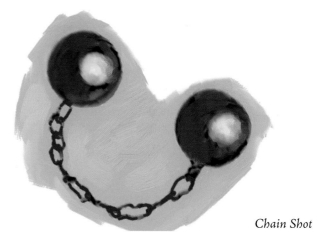

Chain Shot

smoke and overwhelming fumes. Pirates often hoped this strategy would convince the crew to surrender without a fight, allowing them to capture a ship without any damage to prize or booty.

Grenadoes or grenades. Softball-sized hollow containers made of clay, wood, glass, or iron and filled with gunpowder and a variety of sharp objects, or sometimes filled with tar and rags to produce a smokescreen. Each container was topped by a fuse that was lit just before the weapon was launched. The explosion produced shrapnel wounds and often unnerved the crew. Though grenadoes did little damage compared to modern hand grenades, they could nonetheless be very effective in clearing the deck of a ship.

ANTI-PERSONNEL CANNON ROUNDS.

Bundle shot. Short iron bars bundled together with a length of rope. When fired, the bars would begin to spread apart, inflicting serious damage on crew and ship alike at close range.

Grape shot. A small grouping of cast-iron balls wrapped in canvas or burlap. When grape shot was fired its cloth wrapping disintegrated, sending a shower of small shot onto the deck of an enemy ship. It was extremely deadly at close range and was often used to repel unwanted boarders.

Canister or case shot. A box, cage, or metal container filled with nails, stones, musket balls, or other small shot. The canister would open when fired, bombarding the enemy with a deadly array of sharp objects easily capable of penetrating flesh.

Sangrenel. Small bits of jagged scrap iron placed in a canvas or burlap bag. Sangrenel was likely the most feared and deadly of the anti-personnel cannon shot. Like grape shot, its bag disintegrated when it was fired, spraying its victims with metal shards that embedded in the skin and were nearly impossible to remove without even more serious injury.

Pirates were certainly a resourceful lot. They used scrap iron, nails, spikes, stones, and anything else they could get their hands on to feed their cannons. When everything else was gone, they even resorted to using coins. It may be hard to believe—but surgeons are said to have actually cut gold coins out of corpses!

AN IMPRESSIVE ARRAY OF GUNS.

Swivel guns. Small, movable cannons mounted along the rail of a ship. Generally loaded with grape shot, swivel guns were most often used to clear the deck of an enemy vessel at close range or to repel attackers attempting to board a crew's ship.

Musket. Single-shot, long-range gun used to snipe at approaching ships or to repel boarders. Muskets were a favored weapon among early Caribbean buccaneers, who were often said to be the best musket shots in the world. However, the original matchlock muskets were unreliable in wet conditions and took longer to load than the later flintlock variety. The

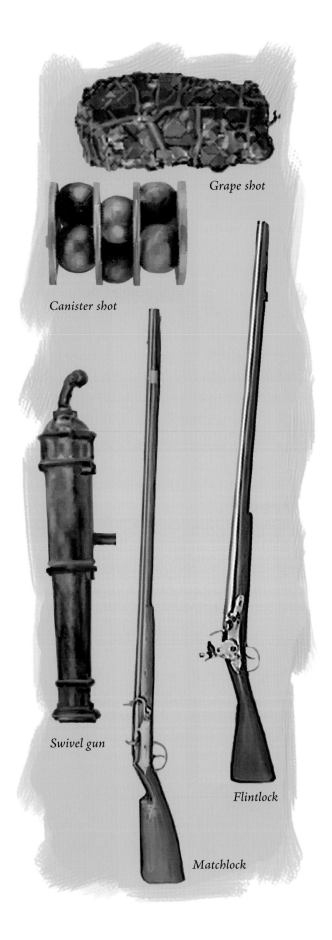

Grape shot

Canister shot

Swivel gun

Matchlock

Flintlock

rifle-style barrel introduced in the 1800s made musket fire more accurate, but it could also be tricky to load. One of the greatest challenges to any marksman was to fire an accurate musket shot while both the ship and his target pitched and rolled on the ocean waves.

Blunderbuss. A short-barrel, muzzle-loading firearm capable of inflicting serious injury at close range. The blunderbuss could be loaded with either small shot or other damaging materials like nails, gravel, or shards of glass. Its funnel-like barrel was believed to help scatter the shot over a wide area. The blunderbuss had a short stock because its tremendous recoil required the gun to be fired from the hip or some other sinewy part of the body. It was primarily used to fend off boarding parties and for personal defense in close combat.

Musketoon. A short-barreled version of the musket rifle. The shoulder-fired musketoon used a scatter shot similar to that of the blunderbuss, but without the latter's vicious kick. One of the chief advantages of the musketoon was that its short barrel allowed for easier use on crowded, rolling decks than that of its longer cousin the musket. Like most other firearms, it was best used at close range.

Flintlock pistol. A lightweight sidearm commonly used from the seventeenth to nineteenth centuries. Single-shot pistols were time-consuming to load, and these small muzzle-loading guns made it easy for pirates to carry more than one. After the gun was fired, the butt end could still have a lethal impact as a club.

Multi-barreled pistol. Muzzle-loading gun that separately fired from two to four rotating or fixed barrels. The firing order was determined by a series of locks and triggers. These pistols were in great demand despite being bulky, costly to make, and often unpredictable.

Pocket pistol. A tiny, easily concealed single-shot weapon. These muzzle-loading flintlock pistols were similar in size to the later Derringer. They would be placed where they could be retrieved quickly and easily and could be deadly at very close range.

Volley gun. Odd-looking, cumbersome pistols that

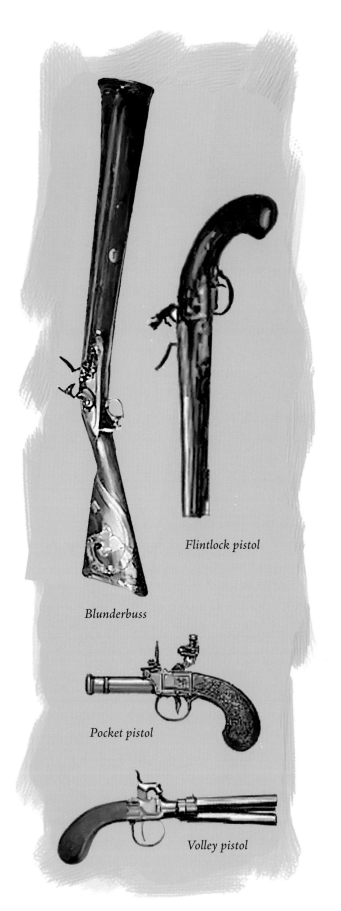

Flintlock pistol

Blunderbuss

Pocket pistol

Volley pistol

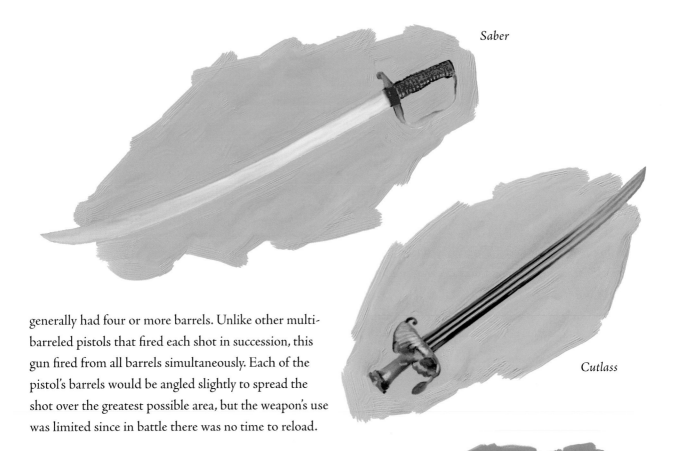

Saber

Cutlass

Dagger

generally had four or more barrels. Unlike other multi-barreled pistols that fired each shot in succession, this gun fired from all barrels simultaneously. Each of the pistol's barrels would be angled slightly to spread the shot over the greatest possible area, but the weapon's use was limited since in battle there was no time to reload.

CLOSE-RANGE WEAPONS:
BLADES AND KNIVES.

Saber. A light dueling or fencing sword with a ta-pered, flexible blade; it had a deadly cutting edge on one side and on the tip.

Cutlass. A broad, medium-length sword with a slightly curved blade sharpened only on the outer edge. The cutlass was the weapon of choice among most seventeenth- and eighteenth-century sailors. Many believe the cutlass evolved from the long knives used by the early buccaneers to butcher meat for their boucans. Their blades were shorter than those of swords or sabers and had a broader, sturdier, curved blade, which made them ideal for fighting in the confined spaces on a ship where longer blades could get tangled in a ship's rigging.

The cutlass was a versatile instrument whose sturdy blade could be used for tasks like hacking down heavy doors, slashing through thick lines, and dividing pieces of eight, as well as for slicing through flesh and bone.

Dagger. A small, multi-purpose knife often used

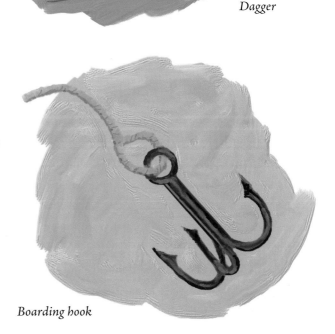

Boarding hook

for cutting sail, rope, or a pirate's dinner, as well as employed in battle. The dagger was small enough to be concealed in a sailor's clothing and was ideal for fighting below decks, where there was little or no room to swing a sword. It had a crossbar or hilt that separated the wielder's hand from the dagger's sharp blade and also offered protection in the event of a sword strike. Unlike the cutlass, whose curved blade could slash through an enemy, the dagger's straight blade was used to thrust and puncture.

Dirk. A type of small dagger designed and used mostly for throwing.

Gully knife. A common single-edged sailor's knife often used for mutiny when nothing else was available.

OTHER NECESSITIES.

Boarding axe. A long-handled axe with sharp and blunt edges at opposite ends of the head. Boarding axes, used during raids to scale the tall sides of wooden ships, were common tools aboard pirate vessels. The sharp blade would bring down masts and rigging or cut the ropes of an enemy's boarding hooks, while the blunt end would shatter doors, hatches, locks—anything that stood between the pirates and their plunder. The handy axes were also an indispensable tool in fighting fires aboard ship, chiseling out hot cannon balls that could ignite a ship's timbers. Though the boarding axe could be useful in close combat, its size and shape did not make it a particularly effective weapon.

Boarding hook. A grappling hook attached to a stout line, used to pull ships closer for boarding.

Scabbard. A scabbard, often highly decorated, housed a sword or knife and kept it clean and sharp.

Bow or crossbow. An early weapon used to incapacitate members of a ship's crew from a distance before boarding. The bow could be difficult to aim on a moving ship, and its use waned with the advent of firearms.

Tomahawk. A small throwing axe popular among pirates of the golden age.

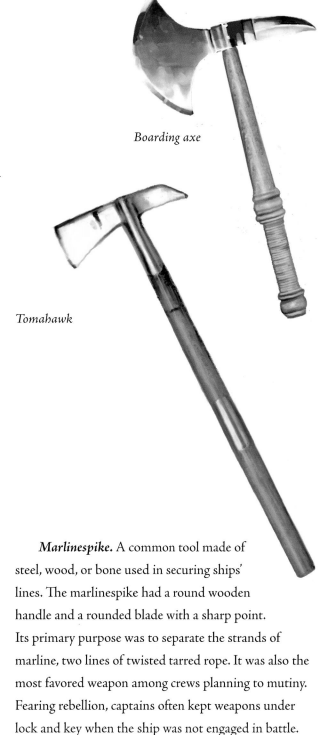

Boarding axe

Tomahawk

Marlinespike. A common tool made of steel, wood, or bone used in securing ships' lines. The marlinespike had a round wooden handle and a rounded blade with a sharp point. Its primary purpose was to separate the strands of marline, two lines of twisted tarred rope. It was also the most favored weapon among crews planning to mutiny. Fearing rebellion, captains often kept weapons under lock and key when the ship was not engaged in battle. Marlinespikes, however, were such necessary tools that they had to remain accessible to the crew.

The Jolly Roger

THE FRENCH PIRATES WHO PLUNDERED the Caribbean islands in the seventeenth century flew a blood-red banner wryly known as *le Joli Rouge*—"the pretty red one." The English sometimes used the term "Old Roger" to refer to the devil. British privateers, starting in 1694, were ordered to fly the Red Jack to signify a legitimate commission from the crown. The pirate flag that developed from these obscure origins struck terror in the hearts of victims, and the sight of the "Jolly Roger" being hoisted on an approaching ship could be sufficient threat to bring about immediate surrender.

At first, pirates employed a variety of national flags or solid colors. But by the 1700s they had begun to incorporate motifs of skeletons, daggers, cutlasses, or bleeding hearts on red or black fields.

Around 1700, **Captain Emanuel Wynne** adopted the first flag commonly associated with piracy. It bore a skull and crossbones over an hourglass, warning his prey that they were on borrowed time. Early in his pirate career Wynne began taking English merchantmen off the Carolina coast; he later moved to the Caribbean.

Each symbol on a pirate flag conveyed a certain message. The skull was a general sign of death, but a skeleton, with or without horns, indicated a tormented death. A violent death was symbolized by a dart or spear, whereas the bleeding heart warned of a slow and painful death. A raised fist or hand clutching a dagger or cutlass implied a general willingness to kill, while an hourglass warned that time was running short—that capture was imminent.

Particular pirates, and most often their intentions, were readily identifiable by the colors and images they chose to display on their flags.

Richard Worley flew a similar flag to that of Emanuel Wynne—a white skull and crossbones centered on a black field. In September 1718, Worley took to plundering along the coast of the American colonies, then headed to the Bahamas. After a few brief successes, he and his crew were captured in February 1719 when they were tricked into attacking two ships sent by the Governor of North Carolina to capture them. After a fierce fight, Worley and one other surviving member of his crew were hanged the following day, bringing a short career of piracy to a fatal end.

Christopher Moody may once have been part of the crew of Black Bart Roberts. Preying on ships off the North and South Carolina coasts between 1713 and 1718, he displayed a skull and crossbones and an hourglass with wings beside a raised, dagger-brandishing arm, signaling "no quarter given"—no lives would be spared. His own life came to an abrupt end on another continent, when he was caught and hanged at Cape Coast Castle in Cabo Corso, Ghana.

Henry Every (or Avery) was one of the first pirates to plunder the Indian Ocean. Serving aboard the Spanish privateer Charles II, in 1694 he led the crew to mutiny over unpaid wages. The newly converted pirate crew elected Every their captain and renamed the ship the Fancy. In ports from Europe to the Americas, the "Arch Pirate" captured so much treasure that he became a hero to the unemployed and destitute throughout England. He flew a black standard, with a profile of a skull wearing an earring and bandana and set over crossed bones. Every lived just long enough to retire with his fortune intact, but he met with difficulty in selling off his appropriated wealth and died in poverty in 1696.

Emanuel Wynne

Richard Worley

Christopher Moody

Henry Every

Walter Kennedy was a mere pickpocket and burglar before he set sail aboard the *Rover* under Capt. Howell Davis in 1718. When Davis was killed in June 1719, Kennedy was appointed second-in-command by the new pirate captain, Bartholomew Roberts. After a raid when Roberts went to investigate a freshly captured vessel, Kennedy absconded with the *Rover*, intending to set a course for Ireland. But he was not much of a navigator, and he instead managed to wreck the ship on the rocky coast of Scotland. Kennedy's pirate flag, featuring the skull and crossbones and an unclothed pirate brandishing sword and hourglass, did not fly for long.

Though most of his crew were captured and hanged, Kennedy escaped to Dublin and eventually to England, where he set up a brothel and engaged in petty crimes. While imprisoned for robbery, the luckless Kennedy was recognized as a pirate—and hanged in 1721.

Thomas Tew, a licensed privateer from Rhode Island, sailed to Bermuda in 1692 and there purchased a share in the sloop *Amity*. He obtained a letter of marque from the royal governor and persuaded his cohorts to join him and the Royal African Company in a raid on the French factory at Goori, in Gambia. Changing course for the Indian Ocean, Tew rounded the Cape of Good Hope and turned to a profitable stint of piracy. In the Red Sea they took an Indian ship that yielded each crew member an astonishing 3,000 pounds.

In Madagascar, Tew met the French captain James Mission, with whom he claimed to have established the utopian pirate colony of Libertalia. Tew's many

Walter Kennedy

Thomas Tew

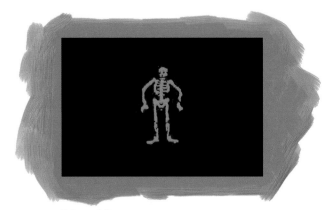

Edward Low

Christopher Condent

escapades carried him back to America and again to the East, where he was killed in 1695 while attacking a heavily armed ship belonging to the Great Mogul of India.

Despite the fearsome sword-arm on his flag, Tew was known for showing mercy; his reputation for comparative kindness earned him many a successful capture.

Edward (Ned) Low was born in London in the late 1600s but came to Boston as a ship rigger. He joined his brother at sea but eventually went out on his own as a pirate, operating mostly along the coast of New England and in the West Indies. Low's reputation for torturing his victims, and for impressing captured sailors into his service, spread far beyond the shores he ravaged.

Low's ensign, a blood-red skeleton on a black background, was gruesomely apt. In one instance, after capturing a Nantucket whaler, Low cut off the commander's ears, sprinkled them with salt, and made the doomed man consume them before he died. In another, Low personally executed fifty-three officers from the captured Spanish galleon *Montcova*, forcing one of the doomed Spanish sailors to eat another's heart before killing him. One day in 1724 his crew, fed up with his brutalities, set him adrift in a small boat without provisions. A French ship rescued Low and took him to the island of Martinique—where he was recognized as a pirate and executed.

Christopher Condent, born in Plymouth, Massachusetts and originally employed as a privateer for England in the War of Spanish Succession, became a sailor and quartermaster aboard a merchant sloop out of New York. Condent was elected captain of the sloop after being wounded in a fight with a vengeful Indian captive who threatened to blow up the ship's powder stores. Upon taking command he raised a pirate banner bearing the triple skull and crossbones and set sail for the Cape Verde Islands.

Condent's exploits were legendary: at the Isle of Mayo boldly engaging an entire fleet of twenty ships; at St. Jago capturing a Dutch privateer that he renamed the *Flying Dragon*; off the coast of Brazil taking number

Jack Rackham

Stede Bonnet

of Portuguese merchant ships. In 1720 he and his crew overtook an Arab vessel carrying a rich cargo for the East India Company. Their fortunes secured, Condent negotiated a pardon from the French governor of the Mascarenes Islands, married the governor's daughter, and renounced his life of piracy. He retired to France a wealthy owner of a fleet of merchant ships.

While many pirates chose simple emblems like Worley's unadorned skull and crossbones or Tew's image of the sword without death, others chose a more complex array of symbols. *Blackbeard's* flag, for example, combined many piratical symbols—a skeleton with horns, an hourglass, a spear, and a bleeding heart. *Calico Jack Rackham's* banner featured a set of crossed swords under a skull to show his willingness to fight. *Stede Bonnet's* emblem, known as the "Pirate Scales" because it represented the balance between life and battle, depicted a skull over a single bone flanked by a heart and a dagger.

Bartholomew (Black Bart) Roberts flew as many as four unique flags. One depicted the pirate toasting, or holding an hourglass with, a spear-wielding skeleton. In Caribbean waters, Roberts flew a different flag to demonstrate his hatred for the islands of Barbados and Martinique. Under a emblem of two skulls appeared initials representing his targets: ABH ("A Barbadian's Head") and AMH ("A Martiniquian's Head"). Roberts got one of his men in 1720, when he hanged the governor of Martinique from a yardarm of his ship.

Pirate flags were an ingenious form of psychological warfare. When pursuing a desired ship, the pirates often flew a white flag hoping the wary captain would "strike her colors," or lower her flag, and surrender. If the ship did not respond, the pirates would raise both the black and white flags to signal their intentions if the victims refused. In the event that a ship did not surrender, the pirates would hoist the red flag, indicating that no quarter would be given and no mercy shown.

A ship could be intimidated into surrender by the mere sight of a swiftly approaching vessel flying the Jolly Roger, especially if its standard belonged to a fearsome foe. When Black Bart Roberts sailed into the harbor at Trepassey, Newfoundland, in June 1720 with his black flags flying, the crews of all twenty-two ships in the harbor abandoned their posts in panic, and Roberts claimed a hefty prize without ever firing a shot.

While a pirate flag undoubtedly convinced many victims that it was useless to resist, flying the Jolly Roger posed some risk for the pirate crew as well. A flag raised too early might scare off the prey with time to escape. But, worse, if the pirates misidentified a potential victim, it could cost them their freedom or even their lives: warships often had standing orders to fire at will on any ship flying a pirate flag.

Blackbeard

Edward England

Bartholomew Roberts

Bartholomew Roberts

Pirate Attire

FOR THE MOST PART, PIRATES WORE the same clothing as other seamen. But they often added articles of stolen clothing and jewelry, especially when going ashore or when going into action.

Pirate dress ran the gamut from the fashion of the times, to the homespun and unadorned, to the extravagant and colorful. Aboard ship pirates frequently went barefooted, saving their shoes for visits ashore.

Though pirates typically employed the same speech as other sailors of their time, a few colorful terms had particular meaning for them.

Pirate Lingo

Pirates spoke the same languages as other people of their nationalities in the same time period. Of course language changes, and the words used by mariners of the Elizabethan era sometimes varied from those used by those of later periods.

Despite Hollywood portrayals, there was no particular pirate "accent"—and not all pirates filled their sentences with "arrgggh" and other popularly attributed forms of pirate speech. As with other professions, pirates did have some specialized terminology, but for the most part pirates would have used terms and sayings that reflected a traditional sailor's vocabulary.

The following words and phrases, while not a complete lexicon, often turn up in pirate writings.

Act of Grace or Act of Pardon. A royal act that provided amnesty to any pirate who promised to cease plundering. Also known as a King's Pardon.

Barnacle. Now used to refer to the marine crustaceans that attach themselves to the wooden hulls of ships, *barnacle* originated as a fourteenth-century name given to a type of goose thought to hatch from the shell of a crustacean because its breeding grounds were unknown.

Belay. To secure a rope by winding it around a cleat or a pin. Belaying pins were located all along the rail of a ship and were used to tie down the ship's rigging. Since they were easily accessible, belaying pins also made excellent weapons. *Belay!* could also serve as a command to stop.

Booty. Derived from a medieval German term that referred to the exchange or distribution of plunder acquired from battle. Over time the word has come to

Corsair. The name given to the Muslim and Christian privateers that terrorized the Mediterranean Sea between the sixteenth and nineteenth centuries. The Muslim, or Barbary, corsairs operated out of ports along the northern coast of Africa. They were sanctioned by the Ottoman Empire to prey on Christian shipping. The Christian corsairs were based on the island of Malta and sailed under orders from the Knights of St. John to attack the "heathen" Turks. Unlike Caribbean privateers, the corsairs did not seek their riches in gold or spices. Instead, they preyed on people and either held their victims for ransom or sold them into slavery.

The term corsair was also used to refer to French privateers operating primarily out of St. Malo, known by the French as La Cité Corsaire.

Dance the hempen jig. A term used by pirates to mean death by hanging. Before 1740, "short drop" hangings were common. Pirates, and other condemned criminals, were forced to climb onto a ladder, stool, or barrel with their hands were tied in front of them. The executioner then placed a dangling noose around their necks and pulled the support out from under them. This led to a cruel death by slow strangulation, and the unfortunate

mean the pillaged plunder itself. Also commonly called loot, plunder, or spoils.

Brethren of the Coast. The name adopted by an organized group of Caribbean buccaneers between 1640 and 1680. Those who belonged to the Brethren adhered to a strict code of conduct known as the Custom of the Coast and agreed not to plunder amongst themselves.

Bumboo. A West Indian beverage made of rum, water, sugar, and nutmeg. It was popular among pirates in the seventeenth and eighteenth centuries, primarily because it had a better taste than the more common grog.

pirate would appear to "dance" on the end of the rope, often made of woven hemp.

Davy Jones's Locker. A fictional realm at the bottom of the ocean that awaited any sailor destined for a watery grave. There are many explanations for the origin of the term. Some believe Davy (or David) Jones was the name of an ill-tempered pub owner who imprisoned drunken sailors in his ale locker and disposed of them on any passing ship. Others believe he is a fiendish spirit of the sea, ruling over all the evil creatures that live there. Still others believe Davy Jones is simply a euphemism for the devil. In all cases, the term struck fear in the hearts of sailors.

"Dead men tell no tales." It is not known whether this phrase was ever actually used by pirates, but it is generally understood to mean that a dead victim was better than a live one, because the dead couldn't testify in court.

Flip. A pirate beverage made of ale, brandy, lemon juice, egg yolk, and sugar and spiced with ginger.

Gibbet. The frame from which the bodies of executed pirates, often enclosed in fitted iron cages, were hung. As a deterrent to those who might choose a life of piracy, the rotting corpses were often left on public display for several weeks.

Grog. Rum mixed with water and lemon juice. It was reportedly introduced in the Royal Navy in 1740 by British Vice-Admiral Edward "Old Grog" Vernon when he ordered his crew's daily ration of rum diluted to resolve problems of drunkenness and lack of discipline.

Inch of candle. Often used to set a time limit on bids during an auction. A one-inch candle was lit when the bidding began, or sometimes a pin was inserted into a larger candle at the one-inch mark before it was lit. As the candle burned down, the bidding proceeded quickly. The one with the highest bid when the flame went out, or when the pin dropped from the candle, became the legal owner of the prize.

Logwood. A small, thorny tree whose unusual trunk resembles a mass of fused stems. The dense hardwood grows in areas along the Yucatan peninsula, and its deep mahogany heartwood was used to produce a rich dye that sold for a handsome price in seventeenth- and eighteenth-century Europe. In the late 1500s the Spanish exported large quantities of logwood from their territories along the Yucatan. By the 1600s the British privateers had discovered the value of the wood and began to capture the Spanish transport ships. When the Spanish navy sent armed escorts to accompany their cargo, the English quickly found it more profitable to illegally harvest the wood themselves.

Mum. A strong beer or ale made from wheat and oat malts and flavored with herbs. It originated in Brunswick, Germany, in the seventeenth century, where it was known as Braunschweiger mumme, and it quickly became popular among western pirates.

Mutiny. Concerted actions of the part of a ship's crew, including refusing to obey orders or participating in active revolt, intended to diminish or withdraw a superior officer's authority.

"No prey, no pay." Pirate crews were compensated with a share of plundered goods, so if they failed to capture prizes they received no pay. Privateers used a similar motto—"No purchase, no pay." The privateers worked for a sort of "commission" and their spoils were "purchased" by the government that commissioned their services, but they too received nothing if they returned to port empty-handed.

No quarter given. Pirates used a system of flags to communicate their intentions to their prospective victims. When approaching another ship, pirates would sometimes fly the Jolly Roger, usually a black flag, as a signal to their prey that their lives would be spared it they surrendered without a fight. If they received no response or the ship refused to surrender, the pirates would raise a red flag, indicating that once the pirates captured the ship, no prisoners would be taken and no mercy, or quarter, would be given.

On the account. Before joining a pirate crew, an person was required to sign the ship's Articles of Agreement. These articles made clear the code of behavior, listed the punishments applicable to specific crimes, and defined the percentage of the profits each person received when a prize was taken. After signing the agreement, each new pirate was asked to place his or her hand on the Bible, a set of crossed pistols or swords, or a human skull and swear an oath of allegiance or honor. Once this was done, the pirate was considered "on the account" and was a full-fledged member of the crew.

Punch house. Originally referring to any low-class drinking establishment, the term was later used by the English as a euphemism for a brothel.

Salmagundi. A popular pirate dish made with a variety of available meats (fish, turtle, chicken, pork, pigeon, and the like) marinated in spiced wine. Hard-boiled eggs, pickled onions, palm hearts, cabbage, grapes, and olives were added to the meat before the whole concoction was seasoned with salt, pepper, garlic, and mustard seed and topped with a vinaigrette dressing. Also known as Solomon Grundy.

Scurvy. A debilitating and eventually fatal disease stemming from a lack of vitamin C that often plagued mariners on long voyages. Also a derogatory term meaning vile, mean, and contemptible when used to describe pirates.

Sea dog. Originally a name for the privateers who attacked Spanish ships and towns under an official sanction from Queen Elizabeth I of England. Now used to describe any experienced sailor.

Soft farewell. Sometimes two or more pirate ships participated in a raid. If the crew of one ship got greedy and wanted to avoid sharing the plunder, they might abscond with the loot under cover of darkness, bidding the others a "soft farewell."

Swashbuckler. A term derived from the antiquated English words "swash," meaning to make a noise by striking, and "buckler," a shield. It first appeared in print around 1560 and was used to describe a mediocre swordsman and braggart who made up for his lack of skill by swaggering through the streets, banging his sword against his shield and challenging passersby to a fight. It is now most often used to refer to the romantic pirates portrayed in adventure novels and Hollywood movies.

Waggoner. A sea atlas or a book of charts and sailing instructions. The book got its name from the Dutch pilot Lucas Waghenaer, who published the first such atlas in 1584. Charts at that time were very expensive, but they were also indispensable on any seagoing vessel—so the waggoner was often a navigator's most closely guarded possession.

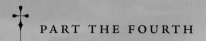

PART THE FOURTH

Rogues & Raiders

PIRATES OF THE GOLDEN AGE

The Adventures of Captain Kidd

DESPITE HIS RELATIVELY SHORT CAREER, Capt. William Kidd was one of the best known pirates of all time. Though originally employed to rid the seas of pirates, the unlucky Kidd himself fell victim to the lure of plundered wealth. The same powers that profited from his successes as a privateer would in time seal his downfall as a pirate.

Kidd was born in England about 1645 and, like many young men of his time, went to sea early. By 1689 he had risen to command of the English privateer *Blessed William*, commissioned to protect the crown's colonies in the Caribbean against French attacks. But in 1690 Kidd's crew mutinied, leaving him stranded on the island of Antigua. In a replacement ship, the *Antigua*, Kidd sailed to New York, where in 1691 he married a widow and settled into the respectable life of a colonial merchant.

But Kidd did not remain on land for long. In 1695 he returned to England, in hopes of securing a privateering commission from King William III. He was not disappointed. His powerful new warship, the *Adventure Galley*, was outfitted with thirty-four cannons and manned by a crew of 150. Under two separate commissions, Kidd was permitted to seize any French vessel and to kill or capture any pirates he encountered.

Before setting sail from England in the late spring

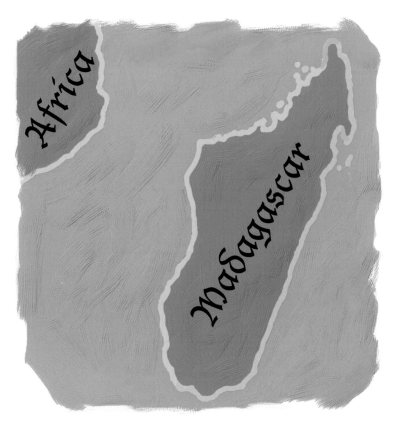

itable pirate ventures. The remainder were on the verge of mutiny—their captain had failed to engage even a single ship! In October, a fight erupted between Kidd and the ship's gunner, William Moore. Kidd killed the man and quelled further talk of mutiny. But Kidd became a different man. He began to plunder any ship he sighted along India's Malabar Coast. The respectable but beleaguered captain had turned pirate.

The holds of the *Adventure Galley* were already filled with ill-gotten riches when Kidd stumbled upon the 400-ton *Quedah Merchant* in January 1698.

The merchant vessel dwarfed Kidd's decaying 284-ton pirate ship. As the pirates approached, the captain of the merchant vessel gave a deceptive sign of surrender—all the while secretly preparing his ship for battle. When the *Adventure Galley* came in range, the merchant vessel opened fire, but a sudden ocean swell caused her shot to go astray. Kidd's crew immediately flung their boarding hooks onto the *Quedah Merchant* and drew alongside. The pirates swarmed aboard the hapless ship, and soon Captain

of 1696, Kidd hand-picked his crew, selecting only those officers he deemed most loyal. Soon after leaving port, however, the *Adventure Galley* was stopped by the HMS *Duchess* and a significant number of Kidd's prized crew were pressed into naval service. Unsatisfied with the group of hardened criminals sent as a replacement, Kidd sailed to New York in September 1696 in search of better recruits. New York, for a brief period in the late 1600s, was a pirate haven, and Kidd departed the city with a seasoned, if less than upstanding, crew.

En route to Madagascar, another mishap befell the ill-fated captain. An outbreak of cholera claimed a third of his ship's crew and Kidd was forced, once again, to take on new sailors. To make matters worse, the *Adventure Galley*, despite its newness, had begun to show signs of rot. Upon reaching the island some of Kidd's men jumped ship to join more prof-

The Adventure Galley

Rumors persist that Capt. Kidd buried treasure in secret places.

Kidd took possession of both ship and booty. The *Quedah Merchant*'s cargo included calico, muslin, silk, and other fabrics as well as brown sugar, opium, iron, and saltpeter. It was one of the greatest pirate treasures ever taken, valued at nearly 50,000 pounds.

With his holds bulging with plunder, Kidd ordered his crew to set course for New York. He made a brief stop for repairs, and to sell off the plundered silk and opium, then sailed as far as St. Mary's Island, where his leaking ship again forced him to land. He grounded the hopeless *Adventure Galley* and transferred her cargo to the captured merchant vessel, which he renamed the *Adventure Prize*.

When Kidd reached the island of Anguilla, he learned that he had been officially declared a pirate, with a price on his head. He sailed on to the island of Hispaniola, where he abandoned the easily recognized *Adventure Prize* and purchased a small sloop, the *Antonio*.

He returned to America, hoping to convince the New York officials that he had taken only the French ships and pirate vessels he was legally sanctioned to capture. But the loot he had tried to sell was too easily recognized as property of the powerful British East India Company.

Kidd was arrested and shipped back to England in chains. The British court sentenced him to death for the murder of William Moore and for piracy on the high seas. Some believe that Kidd was used as a scapegoat by the noble backers who had commissioned his services. The infamous captain swore until his dying moments that he never a pirate.

With the hangman's noose already around his neck, the captain gave a farewell speech memorialized in a popular ditty:

My name was Captain Kidd, When I sail'd, when I sail'd, And so wickedly I did, God's laws I did forbid, When I sail'd, when I sail'd.

I roam'd from sound to sound, And many a ship I found, And then I sunk or burn'd, When I sail'd. I murder'd William Moore, And laid him in his gore, Not many leagues from shore, When I sail'd.

Farewell to young and old, All jolly seamen bold, You're welcome to my gold, For I must die, I must die. Farewell to Lunnon town, The pretty girls all round, No pardon can be found, and I must die, I must die, Farewell, for I must die. Then to eternity, in hideous misery, I must lie, I must lie.

Kidd was as unfortunate in death as he had been in life. The hangman's rope broke twice, and only after a third attempt did he die.

Kidd's body was dipped in tar and hung by chains at Tilbury Point on the Thames River, where it served as a warning against piracy for many years.

The legend of Captain Kidd has endured because of the belief that he hid at least some part of his treasure, though such has yet to be recovered. The tale has been kept alive through such literary works as Edgar Allan Poe's story "The Gold Bug," Robert Louis Stevenson's *Treasure Island*, and Nelson DeMille's *Plum Island*. Treasure hunters for more than three centuries have been inspired to search places like Oak Island, Nova Scotia; Gardiner's Island in New York; and several islands along the New England shore and rivers. There have even been rumors of his treasure being buried somewhere on the Carolina coast.

While Captain Kidd is known to have buried a small cache at Cherry Tree Field on New York's Long Island Sound, it was retrieved before his death and sent to England to be used as evidence against him in the trial that determined his fate as a pirate.

New York in Captain Kidd's day

Blackbeard, Terror of the Seas

EDWARD TEACH, EDWARD THATCH, and Edward Drummond are all aliases of the most famous of all pirates—known as Blackbeard. Born in Bristol, England, on November 23, 1675, the notorious marauder lasted only two short years in piracy before he was captured and killed. But his fearsome reputation persists to the current day.

Blackbeard was an imposing figure—broad at the shoulder, exceedingly strong, and standing well over six feet tall. His coal-black beard, braided in coarse untamed strands tied with colored ribbon, covered nearly the whole of his face. The swords he kept strapped to his waist and the bandoliers laden with pistols and knives that crisscrossed his garish crimson coat further enhanced the self-proclaimed commodore's menacing appearance.

While the very sight of Blackbeard may have been enough to persuade his victims to surrender without a fight, his reputation as a devilish fiend was even more alarming. He was known to intimidate his enemies by weaving long matches or gunpowder-coated cannon fuses coated into his hair and setting them alight during battles. He often threatened his terrified hostages with horrifying, torturous deaths; legend has it that he once shot his own first mate in order to prove his mettle. Rumor even spread that he had as many as fourteen wives—and killed them all.

Despite Blackbeard's barbarous reputation, there is no evidence to suggest he ever killed any of his prey. To the contrary, if a ship surrendered peacefully, his hard-driven pirates plundered the vessel's weapons, rum, navigational instruments, and any valuable cargo aboard—then allowed both ship and crew to sail away unharmed. If a particularly bold target resisted, Blackbeard would simply maroon the unfortunate sailors and burn the ship, leaving fate to determine the outcome.

Like many of his piratical contemporaries, Edward Teach began his seagoing life as a privateer during the War of Spanish Succession. When the war ended, many unemployed privateers turned to piracy. Teach joined the marauding crew of his former mentor, Captain Benjamin Hornigold.

In 1716 Hornigold gave Teach command of his first ship, a small six-gun sloop with a crew of seventy-five men. The following fall, the two captured a twenty-six gun, wealth-laden French slave ship, the *Concorde*, off the Caribbean coast of St. Vincent. As a reward for his strength, courage, and leadership, Hornigold gave com-

mand of the newly acquired prize to his able apprentice.

When King George I of England extended full amnesty to any pirate who ceased to plunder, Hornigold accepted the offer and retired from piracy. Teach, however, wanted no part of the king's pardon. Instead, he sailed on without his mentor, making the Dutch-built *Concorde* his flagship. The freebooting Blackbeard immediately increased his ship's strength to forty guns and rechristened her the *Queen Anne's Revenge*.

Soon after, the fledgling captain met Stede Bonnet, known as "The Gentleman Pirate" because of his history as a wealthy, educated landowner on the island of Barbados. So amused was Blackbeard by the dandy captain's proper demeanor that he invited Bonnet, with his ten-gun sloop the *Revenge*, to join his flotilla.

However, within only a few days the seasoned Blackbeard realized that Bonnet was an inept sailor at best, unaccustomed to the rigors of pirate life and lacking in fortitude and leadership skills. Blackbeard persuaded the dainty Bonnet to join him as a guest aboard the *Queen Anne's Revenge* and put another pirate, a lieutenant named Richards, in command of the smaller *Revenge*. Bonnet remained a virtual prisoner aboard Blackbeard's flagship until it ran aground six months later.

During the winter of 1717–18, the two ships cruised the warm Caribbean waters, commandeering the riches of as many as twelve ships. Blackbeard added two small captured vessels, including the Jamaican sloop *Adventure*, to his entourage. In the spring of 1718, the pirates sailed north up the coast of the American colonies with their captain in command of four ships and more than three hundred pirates.

As perhaps his most brazen exploit, Blackbeard's small flotilla took the crews of several ships entering the port of Charleston, South Carolina, hostage during a week-long blockade in May of 1718. His crew was short of medical stores, and Blackbeard demanded provisions from the local government as ransom. Much to the dismay and indignation of the city's inhabitants, Blackbeard's pirates roamed freely about the streets of Charleston while they awaited an answer. When the council delivered a chest of medical supplies valued at between 300 and 400 pounds, Blackbeard released his prisoners and their looted ships, and he and his cohort sailed north.

*Governor Spottiswood
of Virginia*

Queen Anne's Revenge

Pirates were a greedy bunch, and Blackbeard was no exception. He devised a cunning plan to cheat all but a few of his most loyal men out of their share of the booty. A week after leaving Charleston, Blackbeard purposely ran the *Queen Anne's Revenge* aground at Beaufort Inlet, North Carolina. Blackbeard's trusted captain aboard

the *Adventure* feigned an attempt to set the flagship free, stranding the small sloop as well.

With the two ships out of commission, Blackbeard marooned twenty-five unhappy pirates on a narrow sandbar before relieving Bonnet's *Revenge* of her wealthy cargo and making off with most of their accumulated riches aboard his remaining small vessel.

Bonnet, free of Blackbeard's hospitality, rescued the marooned sailors and returned to his own piratical career aboard the *Revenge*, subsequently renamed the *Royal James*.

Blackbeard, with his small, hand-picked crew and substantial ill-gotten plunder, sailed up the coast to Bath, the capital of North Carolina at that time. Every one of the pirates received pardons from Gov. Charles Eden, who is thought to have shared in Teach's spoils.

But Blackbeard and his pirates soon returned to their illegal trade. Virginia's Gov. Alexander Spottswood grew weary of the raids and dispatched a Royal Navy contingent, including two powerful men-o'war, the *Pearl* and the *Lime*, to North Carolina in search of the insolent rogue.

The naval detachment, under the command of Lt. Robert Maynard, surprised the sleeping pirate captain at Ocracoke Inlet, North Carolina, on November 22, 1718. In the bloody battle that ensued, Blackbeard reportedly sustained more than twenty sword lacerations and severe wounds from five musket rounds before he perished. Lieutenant Maynard and his escort returned to Virginia victorious, with Blackbeard's severed head swinging from the bowsprit of the *Pearl*.

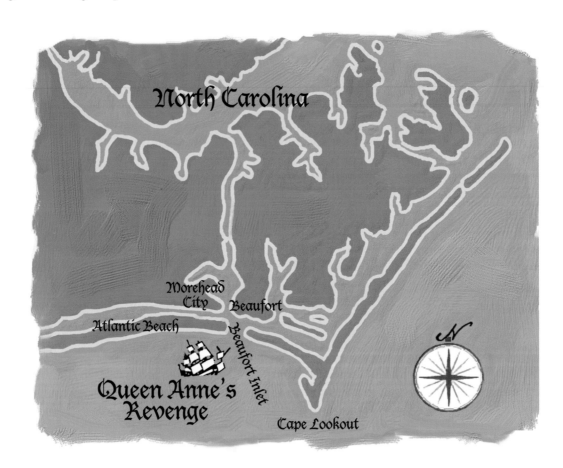

Stede Bonnet, a Most Unusual Pirate

STEDE BONNET WOULD HAVE TO BE considered the most unlikely of all pirates. A well-educated retired army major and wealthy sugar plantation owner from Barbados, he had absolutely nothing in common with the ruthless seagoing raiders of his day. Bonnet's genteel life centered around the most respected, most affluent segment of polite Bridgetown society. He was in all ways a gentleman—from his powdered wig, satin vest, and lace-cuffed shirt to his cultured background and impeccably refined manners. Perhaps most peculiar of all, he had virtually no knowledge of the sea.

So what could possibly prompt such a well-bred landlubber to take to the villainous life of a pirate raider? Some believe it was a mental disorder or disenchantment with the excesses of society life. Others say it was the constant vexation of a nagging wife.

Whatever the reason, Bonnet's seafaring career was anything but ordinary from the very start. He embarked on his new endeavor by legally purchasing, rather than stealing or capturing, a ship—an insufferable affront to any respectable pirate. Bonnet named his ten-gun sloop the *Revenge* and recruited seventy destitute seamen from the taverns and grog shops of Bridgetown for her crew. Unlike other pirate captains, Bonnet did not require his men to sign a contract or swear an oath. Apparently unaware of standard piratical practice, he also paid them from his own pocket. Imagine, salaried pirates! Of course, this strategy would prove beneficial to Bonnet, since it would soon keep the inept captain from facing mutiny by his disillusioned crew.

To his Bridgetown contemporaries, Bonnet explained that he had purchased the small vessel in order to trade with the neighboring islands. For several days the ship sat moored in the Bridgetown harbor, until one night, without a word to friend or family, Bonnet ordered his crew to weigh anchor, and the pirate ship *Revenge* set sail for Virginia.

On his first adventure as a rogue outlaw, Bonnet's crew managed to capture four vessels despite their captain's ignorance of seafaring lore—the Scottish *Anne*, the English *Endeavor* and *Young*, and the *Turbes* out of Barbados. While the pirates only plundered the first three ships, Bonnet ordered the last one, and every subsequent Barbadian ship they captured, burned, in a futile attempt to keep news of his piratical ways from reaching his home.

But Bonnet's men had begun to take notice of his incompetence, and hostile whispers could be heard among the crew. After a brief trek up the New England coast, the pirates turned south and headed for the Bay of Honduras. There Bonnet encountered the *Queen Anne's Revenge*, captained by one of the most feared pirates of all times, Blackbeard. Strangely enough, the two seemingly incompatible pirate captains quickly became friends and decided it would be more profitable to sail in consort rather than alone.

When Blackbeard learned of his new comrade's inexperience, he insisted that Bonnet move to more comfortable and spacious living quarters on the *Queen Anne's Revenge*. He suggested that a man of Bonnet's refined nature should spend his time reading—Bonnet

had his personal library delivered aboard the *Revenge* before he set sail—and wandering freely about the deck. Bonnet should not be encumbered by rigors to which he was unaccustomed, his host explained.

As an involuntary guest on Blackbeard's ship, Bonnet often did wander the deck, sometimes dressed only

A pirate party

in his morning gown. Blackbeard placed one of his own officers in command of the *Revenge*. Confidence in the new lieutenant's ability, as well as stern discipline, soon quelled any further threat of mutiny. It was six months before Bonnet regained command of the *Revenge*—and only after Blackbeard had absconded with most of their combined riches.

Again in control of his ship and crew, Bonnet sailed to Bath, North Carolina, where he turned himself in to Gov. Charles Eden and asked for an official pardon.

Pardon in hand, however, Bonnet changed his name to Captain Thomas (and later to Captain Edwards), rechristened his ship the *Royal James*, and returned to piracy.

Today, only a few miles down the coast from Wilmington, North Carolina, lies the mouth of the Cape Fear River, and a quaint little town called Southport. A narrow road parallels the river heading north from the town center. It crosses a small creek after a short distance.

Beside the road stands a small marker with a metal plaque bearing the following inscription:

"BONNET'S CREEK . . . Stede Bonnet, the 'Gentleman Pirate', used the mouth of this creek as a hide-out for his vessel, the *Royal James*, formerly called *Revenge*. Here on September 26, 1718, the great Battle of the Sand Bars was fought between the pirates and the men sent to capture them under the command of Col. William Rhett aboard the *Henry* and *Sea Nymph*. After a twenty-four hour battle there were nineteen men killed, twenty-three wounded, and Bonnet, with the remains of his pirate crew, surrendered. On November 8, 1718, twenty-nine pirates were hanged in Charleston, S.C."

A few weeks later, holding a cluster of flowers in his manacled hands, gentleman Stede Bonnet met the same fate on the gallows.

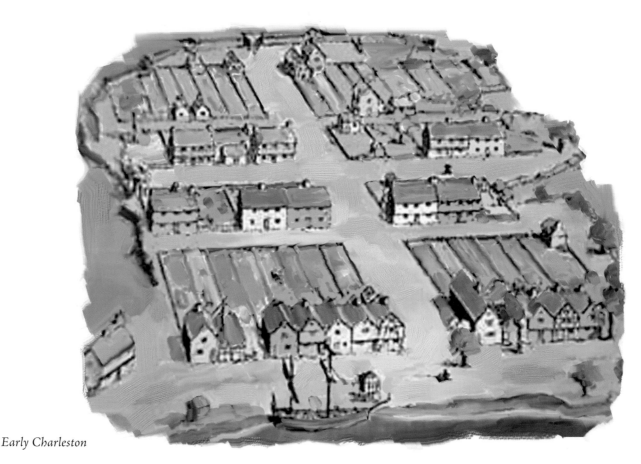

Early Charleston

Samuel Bellamy and the Whydah

Samuel Bellamy, like Blackbeard, got his start in the pirate trade sailing under Benjamin Hornigold. In 1716 Bellamy was elected captain after Hornigold, refusing to loot British ships, departed.

Bellamy cruised in the company of other pirates for the next year, leaving a vast treasure for future generations to locate. With Olivier La Bouche he seized several ships near the Virgin Islands. Bellamy kept one of the large ships and transferred his sloop to the command of Paul Williams, with whom he operated between Haiti and Cuba. In March Bellamy and Williams captured the *Whydah*, a slave ship loaded with gold, sugar, ivory, and indigo. Sailing north to Virginia, they took at least four more ships. They were thrown off course in a storm but captured several more vessels as they headed for Rhode Island. Two of their ships, including the *Whydah*, wrecked during a heavy fog on the night of May 17, 1717 at Orleans, Massachusetts. Bellamy lost his life that night, surviving to enjoy none of the fruits of his efforts.

The *Whydah* reportedly carried a cargo valued at 20,000 pounds worth of cargo. In the mid-1980s, divers off Cape Cod recovered part of Bellamy's booty—a find worth millions of dollars by then.

The Fortunes of Black Bart Roberts

BARTHOLOMEW "BLACK BART" ROBERTS was easily the most successful pirate of the golden age. During his brief but bloody four-year career he reportedly captured more than 400 ships and amassed more than 50,000,000 pounds in plundered wealth and cargo.

By all accounts, Roberts was an uncommon pirate. He often dressed in a garish crimson waistcoat and gentleman's breeches, with a red feather tucked in the brim of his tricorn hat. A silk bandolier draped across his shoulder held a brace of readied pistols, while a diamond-studded cross hung from his neck by a length of gold chain. A pious man, the captain regularly conducted religious services aboard his ship and refused to plunder on the Sabbath. Roberts was also a teetotaler, a truly unusual quality for a pirate, and he forbade drinking and gambling among his crew.

But in spite of his gentlemanly appearance and deceptive religious bent, Black Bart had a dark side—

he was the most menacing and brutal pirates ever to sail the Seven Seas.

Born John Roberts in southern Wales around 1682, he went to sea as a ship's cabin boy at age thirteen. By 1719 he was serving as third mate aboard the British slaver *Princess* off the coast of Ghana. When Roberts's ship was captured by pirate captain Howell Davis, he reluctantly joined the marauding crew.

Roberts adopted the name Bartholomew shortly after joining Davis's crew. Within a month, he proved his worth as an able sailor and Davis took him under his wing. However, Davis was soon killed during an attempt to abduct the governor of the island of Principe.

Following Davis's death, Roberts was elected captain of the *Royal Rover*. His first official act was to return to Principe, ransacking and butchering.

With his mentor's death avenged, Black Bart and his men set sail for Brazil. In the harbor of Todos Os Santos' Bay, they encountered forty-two Portuguese trading vessels and their two seventy-gun escorts preparing for a voyage to Lisbon. The pirates stealthily boarded one of the larger wealth-laden ships and made off with vast stores of sugar, furs, tobacco, and jewels—and 40,000 gold coins. By the time the two warships realized what had happened, Roberts and his crew were on their way to Devil's Island off the African coast to sell their newly acquired booty.

One of Roberts's crew, Walter Kennedy, later absconded with the seventy-gun *Royal Rover* and its remaining 30,000 pounds of gold. Left with only a captured ten-gun sloop, the *Fortune*, an indignant but undaunted Captain Roberts weighed anchor and headed north up the Atlantic coast.

Kennedy's treacherous act inspired Roberts to pen his famous pirate articles—a strict set of rules which all crew members had to follow, but which made life aboard

Black Bart's crews plundered fifteen French and British ships in one three-day period.

Roberts's ship remarkably fair and democratic. By June 1720, the *Fortune* was terrorizing the eastern coast of Newfoundland, attacking seagoing traffic as well as the major ports of Ferryland and Trepassey. In a period of less than nine months, the industrious pirates seized or destroyed more than two dozen sloops and some 150 fishing boats.

Outside the ravished Trepassey harbor, the pirates encountered a flotilla of nine French trading ships. After looting the ships and torturing many of the sailors, Roberts transferred his stolen goods to a twenty-eight-gun brigantine which became his new flagship, the *Good Fortune*.

Realizing that it was unwise for a pirate to remain in one place for too long, Roberts and his greedy crew charted a course south, plundering fifteen French and English ships in a three-day period off the island of St. Kitts before arriving in French Martinique in January 1721. In a fiendishly ingenious ploy,

pounds. To make up for the loss of the *Good Fortune*, Roberts kept the *Onslow* as a prize, renaming her the *Royal Fortune*—the fourth and last of his ships to carry that name.

In early January 1722, off Africa's Ivory Coast, Roberts captured a thirty-two gun French warship which he renamed the *Great Ranger*. On January 11, he seized eleven slave ships near Whydah that he held for a ransom of eight pounds of gold dust each. When one of the Portuguese captains refused to pay the required sum Roberts burned his ship, with eighty slaves still alive and trapped in the vessel's cargo hold.

News of Black Bart's raids and atrocities continued to spread. British trading companies were suffering tremendous losses, and many placed handsome bounties on his head. Pirate hunters smelled hefty profits—and they were out for his blood.

On February 5, 1722, Capt. Challoner Ogle, in command of the sixty-gun British warship HMS *Swallow*, sighted Roberts's flotilla near Cape Lopez, Gabon. Some records indicate that Roberts mistook Ogle's ship for an innocent merchant vessel; others show that his crew may simply have been drunk after a successful raid the previous day. On February 10, Black Bart and his crew were unprepared for the *Swallow*'s swift attack.

Following a single barrage of grapeshot, Bartholomew Roberts was found dead, slumped over a cannon with a gaping hole in his throat. According to their beloved captain's wishes, the reportedly tearful pirate crew tossed Black Bart's lifeless body overboard to prevent it from being displayed on a public gallows.

After a two-hour battle, the demoralized crew was forced to surrender. They were tried for piracy at the Cape Coast Castle in Ghana. Seventy-four crew members were acquitted, seventy African pirates were hanged, and thirty-seven received lesser sentences. Black Bart would capture ships and torture sailors no more.

the sadistic pirate captain sent word to the island of a fictitious slave sale in neighboring St. Lucia. He then lay in wait, ambushing all fourteen French ships that responded to the trap. Roberts once again added to his fleet by taking an eighteen-gun brigantine he renamed *Good Fortune*.

Bart earned his "Black" reputation by severely torturing and killing many of the French prisoners. Some were brutally whipped or had their ears cut off; others were hanged and their bodies used for target practice.

While still in Caribbean waters, Roberts captured a fifty-two gun man-o'-war which he renamed the *Royal Fortune*. Much to his delight, one of the warship's passengers was the governor of Martinique. Black Bart took great pleasure in hanging the unfortunate Frenchman from the yardarm of his new flagship.

With his cargo holds filled with the riches of nearly 100 plundered vessels and Caribbean shipping almost at a standstill because of his exploits, Roberts set sail for West Africa to sell his ill-gotten spoils.

By August Roberts and his crew were off the coast of Liberia, where they captured the *Onslow*, a Royal Africa Company frigate carrying cargo worth nearly 9,000

Calico Jack and the Lady Pirates

John "Calico Jack" Rackham is perhaps better known for the distinctive fabric of his clothing and for his relation to history's two most famous female pirates than for his own dubious piratical prowess.

In November of 1718, while serving as quartermaster aboard the pirate ship *Treasure*, Rackham openly accused Capt. Charles Vane of cowardice for failing to attack a French warship despite the wishes of his crew to do so. Mutiny followed, and Vane, along with a small contingent of supporters, was set adrift in an unarmed sloop. Aboard the *Treasure*, the remaining pirates elected the outspoken Rackham their new leader.

However, after a few months of successful plundering, Rackham decided to abandon the pirate life and sailed for the Bahamian island of New Providence, where he received an official pardon from Gov. Woodes Rogers in May 1719. While still on the island, the pardoned pirate made the acquaintance of Anne Bonny, a fiery young redhead with a passion that dwarfed his own.

Bonny was born in County Cork, Ireland, the illegitimate daughter of prominent attorney William Cormac and a housemaid by the name of Peg, or Mary, Brennan. To cover the couple's indiscretion young Anne was disguised as a boy apprenticed to her father's legal service. But Cormac's wife discovered the truth, and the public scandal that followed

Calico Jack's nickname came from his distinctive style of dress.

destroyed his legal career.

With all hopes of a future in Ireland devastated, Cormac sailed for the American colonies, taking Anne and her mother with him. In Charleston, South Carolina, he again prospered—as a lawyer, a merchant, and eventually a wealthy plantation owner. When her mother died Anne became mistress of the household. Her father's wealth made her an attractive catch among Charleston's elite.

But the budding young woman proved more than a handful. At thirteen she reportedly stabbed a servant girl in the belly with a table knife, and she later beat a young man so brutally for making unwanted advances that his injuries kept him bedridden for weeks.

Anne was ultimately disinherited when, still in her teens, she eloped with a poor young sailor named James Bonny against her father's wishes. With any future inheritance lost, the young couple headed for the West

Indian island of New Providence to seek their fortune.

Anne Bonny was fascinated by the island's rough inhabitants and frequented many of the pirate-infested waterfront bars. Meanwhile, her husband had become a spy for privateer captain, and later governor, Woodes Rogers, earning his living by denouncing as a pirate any sailor he happened not to like. Anne soon tired of her stool-pigeon husband and fell for a dashing young pirate known as Calico Jack. When the affair between Jack and his married lover became public, Governor Rogers threatened to have Anne flogged for adultery. Rather than risk the punishment, Rackham stole a sloop and returned to piracy, taking Anne with him.

A few months out Anne became pregnant, and Jack took her to stay with friends in Cuba. After their child's birth the determined lady pirate rejoined her adventurous lover at sea. The baby's fate remains unknown.

Shortly after Anne's return, several crew members

Mary Read

aboard a captured Dutch ship were pressed into joining Rackham's pirates. One in particular caught Anne's attention—a handsome young blond-haired, blue-eyed English boy. Only the boy was not a boy at all. He was instead a young woman named Mary Read.

Unlike Anne, Mary spent most of her life disguised as a boy. She was the illegitimate daughter of a London sailor's wife whose husband had been at sea for more than a year when she born. Mary's mother dressed her as a boy to impersonate her deceased but legitimate older brother who had died in infancy. It was the only way the desperate mother could continue to collect the monthly stipend provided by the boy's paternal grandmother.

At age thirteen, after the death of her grandmother, Mary was apprenticed as a footboy to a wealthy Frenchwoman. But the adventurous lass soon ran away to sea, signing on as cabin boy aboard a man-o'-war only to jump ship a few years later and become a foot soldier in the War of Spanish Succession.

Mary Read later transferred to a cavalry regiment, where she met and fell in love with a fellow soldier. She anxiously revealed her true gender, and the couple were later married. When the two opened a tavern called the Three Horseshoes near Breda, Holland, Mary lived openly as a woman for the first time in many years.

Unfortunately, young Mary's husband died soon thereafter, and the tavern failed. Realizing that life was easier for a man, she once again donned her masculine disguise and returned to life in the infantry. But a brief period of peace gave way to boredom, and Read soon shipped out as a sailor aboard a Dutch merchant vessel bound for the West Indies.

When the ill-fated ship was captured by Rackham's pirates, Read, the sole English sailor aboard, was invited to join the pirate crew. Thus began the young woman's career as a pirate—and her intriguing affiliation with Anne Bonny and Calico Jack Rackham.

Unaware of Mary's disguise, Anne revealed her own gender and began making sexual advances toward the handsome young sailor. Mary was forced to reveal the truth, and the two quickly became close friends. But Jack was convinced that his fiery mistress had taken a new lover and threatened to slit Mary's throat. Anne quickly told Rackham of Mary's true identity.

The two fierce female pirates proved to be skillful and blood-thirsty raiders. Never shrinking from a fight, they were as willing to board an well-armed man-o'-war or murder their hapless victims any of the men in Rackham's crew.

However, their short-lived piratical careers came to an end in November of 1720 when pirate hunter Capt. Jonathan Barnett surprised Rackham's drunken crew as they lay anchored off Jamaica's north coast. The women fought bravely in the brief battle, but in the end the pirates surrendered.

Captain Barnett testified before a Jamaican court that only two of Rackham's pirates had put up much resistance. With pistols, cutlasses, and boarding axes the two fought like banshees before they were finally subdued. He reported that one of the two fierce pirates even fired into their own ship's hold, where the rest of the crew was hiding, and screamed for them to come up and fight like men. The court was surprised to learn that the two courageous pirates were women.

In a separate trial Anne Bonny and Mary Read were

sentenced to hang along with John Rackham and the rest of the convicted pirates. When the judge asked if any of the condemned had anything further to say, the pair replied, "Milord, we plead our bellies." The judge found himself confronted with two pregnant pirates.

By law the court could not take the life of an unborn child by executing the mother—so both Anne and Mary were imprisoned pending the delivery of their respective children. It appears that neither of the lady

pirates were ever hanged. Mary died in prison before giving birth and Anne simply disappeared—perhaps paroled through her father's influence.

One contemporary source gives the trial testimony thus:

"The two women, prisoners at the bar, were then on board the said sloop, and wore men's jackets, and long trousers, and handkerchiefs tied about their heads; and that each of them had a machete and pistol in their hands,

and cursed and swore at the men, to murder the deponent; and that they should kill her, to prevent her coming against them; and the deponent further said, that the reason of her knowing and believing them to be women then was by the largeness of their breasts.

Another witness stated the women were very active on board, and that Ann Bonny handed gunpowder to the men; also, 'that when they saw any vessel, gave chase, or attacked, they wore men's clothes; and at other times, they wore woman's clothes.'"

The verdict was summarily handed down on November 17, 1721:

"You, Mary Read, and Ann Bonny, alias Bonn, are to go from hence to the place from whence you came, and from thence to the place of execution; where you shall be severally hanged by the neck till you are severally dead. And god of his infinite mercy be merciful to both your souls."

Calico Jack asked to see Anne Bonny one last time as he was escorted to the gallows at a place now called Rackham's Cay near the once prosperous Port Royal, Jamaica. With a scornful glance the intrepid female pirate bid farewell to her doomed lover, declaring, "Had you fought like a man, you need not have been hanged like a dog."

Calico Jack suffered the same fate as many captured pirates.

A Spanish galleon

Charles Vane, Defiant Holdout

OF THE EARLY CAREER OF CHARLES VANE little is known. A tale of one particularly cunning exploit that has come down to this day involves an early eighteenth-century Spanish galleon that was wrecked in shallow water off the Florida coast. Many pirates fought over the site, but they were driven off by Spanish warships guarding the site. Vane had a better plan: he conserved his resources and waited for the Spanish to recover their own riches from the wreck. He then way-laid the recovering ship—and seized one of the richest prizes in pirate history.

Vane rose to prominence at about the same time

Charles Vane

that Woodes Rogers assumed the governorship of the Caribbean island of New Providence in July 1718. Governor Rogers offered pardons to those pirates who would turn themselves in. Vane was one of the few who defiantly refused to accept the pardon.

It was Vane himself who delayed Rogers's arrival in New Providence, when he a ship afire and sent it into the British frigate *Rose.* Vane then raised sail and escaped from of the harbor with a ship full of plunder. The angry governor sent Capt. Benjamin Hornigold, himself a notorious former pirate, to track down the defiant pirate. But Vane eluded capture and for much of the following three years ranged freely. At one point he commanded a fleet of three ships.

Vane put a pirate named Yeats in charge of one captured sloop, and the two ships made for the South Carolina coast together to practice their evil craft. Just as Blackbeard had done earlier, Vane made several captures outside Charles Town (Charleston), but his crew began to grumble when Vane evaded other ships they considered worthy of plunder. Yeats, deciding to be his own captain, bid Vane a "soft farewell," stealthily departing in the middle of the night. Taking with him with some of the plunder and slaves from a recently captured brig, Yeats and his crew sailed for Charleston, where they surrendered and accepted the British pardon.

By September 1718 the governor of South Carolina had grown impatient with the predations of the pirates and dispatched two armed sloops led by Col. William Rhett to capture Vane. Colonel Rhett, misled by misinformation the wily Vane had given surviving sailors, failed to track Vane but by chance came upon "the gentleman pirate," Stede Bonnet—whom he successfully outmaneuvered and captured.

Vane's elusive trip north eventually led him to a week-long party with Blackbeard on North Carolina's Ocracoke Island. In early October Vane sailed up the coast toward New York, but by late November had taken only a few meager prizes. On November 23, off New Jersey, Vane exchanged fire with an unknown ship. When the vessel was discovered to be a French warship and Vane elected not to pursue it, his crew accused him of cowardice and elected the quartermaster, Calico Jack Rackham, as their new captain.

Vane and his supporters were provided with a small sloop and set out for an area of the Caribbean Sea between Jamaica and the Yucatan. In those waters, for a few weeks, they had some success plundering various vessels. In February 1719, while en route to the Windward Passage, they ran into a hurricane. Vane's two sloops were wrecked on an uninhabited island in the Bay of Honduras, and almost all the crew were drowned. Only Vane and one other of his former crew managed to survive by eating turtles and fish.

The first ship to come upon the stranded pair was an old acquaintance, Captain Holford—but Holford did not trust Vane and refused to take him aboard. The hapless pirates were soon rescued by another vessel. Shortly after they left the island, however, an encounter with Captain Holford's ship led to the discovery of Vane's identity. He was taken prisoner and turned over to the authorities in Jamaica.

On March 22, 1720, Charles Vane was swiftly tried and hanged in Port Royal, Jamaica, at Gallows Point, his body left to hand in chains at Gun Cay as a warning to any others who refused to follow the law.

Shipwrecked!

Other Pirates, Other Times

PIRATES OF OTHER LANDS AND CENTURIES

Jean Lafitte

Jean Lafitte: Pirate or Patriot?

JEAN LAFITTE WAS A LATECOMER on the pirate stage. True, piracy might thrive in any part of the world where commerce flourished—but by the turn of the nineteenth century pirates had largely been routed from the Atlantic and the Caribbean.

This curious fellow of French ancestry is hard to judge. Was he a cutthroat pirate, a patriotic privateer, or a gentleman rover? The answer still eludes the historical authorities. One thing is clear: Lafitte made an important contribution to the United States in a time of the young nation's peril.

Jean Lafitte's place of birth and place of death remain mysteries. According to some accounts he was born in the former colony of St. Domingue; others claim he hailed from the city of Bayonne, or perhaps Bordeaux, in France. He may have died—still a pirate—in the Yucatan in the mid 1820s, or he may have lived on as an honest middle-class American citizen into the 1850s.

Sometime around 1803 Lafitte turned up in the Gulf of Mexico, preying on shipping. Operating from the desolate swamps of Barataria, on the coast of Louisiana, he sold smuggled slaves and pilfered merchandise. In the bustling port city of New Orleans, where his older brother Pierre openly sold slaves through notaries, Jean Lafitte demonstrated his arrogance to the authorities, "parading arm-in-arm on the streets of New Orleans with his buddies." When any of his cohorts were arrested for piracy, his crafty lawyers who always managed to get them out of jail. (His tactics came up short once in 1814, when Pierre spent a sweltering summer in chains.)

Lafitte and his compatriots, operating what a Ger-

Andrew Jackson

man merchant described as a "colony of pirates" infesting the shores of Louisiana, were all surprised and taken captive by federal agents in September 1814 at Grand Terre Island.

A short time later, Lafitte refused a handsome offer from a British navy captain to join the ongoing War of 1812 on the British side. He instead offered his troops to aid Gov. William Claiborne on the American side. Lafitte received a curt refusal and proceeded to extend his offer to Gen. Andrew Jackson. Lafitte and his pirates were welcomed into the ragtag American army being assembled by General Jackson.

Galveston

New Orleans

Gulf of Mexico

Jackson's troops sorely needed flints and gunpowder, and Lafitte handily provided them from his stolen stores in Barataria. Lafitte's pirates joined with Jackson's small body of American Marines, soldiers and volunteers in the great Battle of New Orleans on January 8, 1815. Along with Jackson's Kentucky and Tennessee sharpshooters, Lafitte's backwoods marksmen on that wintry morning helped to trounce the advancing British army and win one of America's greatest victories.

Jean Lafitte received a pardon for his whole company and for a year or so afterwards walked the streets of New Orleans a free man. But Lafitte had larceny in his blood, and he could not stand to live within the law for long. Quitting New Orleans for the frontier of Texas, he established a new community of smugglers and a new base for privateering on Galveston Island. When the

American government eventually got serious about his activities and drove him out of the region, he moved on to the Yucatan Peninsula—where he vanished from the pages of history for many years.

In the 1940s a document purporting to be Jean Lafitte's journal surfaced, among family papers in a old trunk inherited by a purported descendant.

According to the journal, Lafitte had lived until the 1850s and died a prosperous, law-abiding citizen. Lafitte remains an enigma. Was he a pirate, or was he a patriot? Perhaps he was both.

The Battle of New Orleans, January 8, 1815

Barbary Corsairs: Scourge of the Mediterranean

To most Westerners, the word "pirate" usually conjures up images of raiders from Europe and the Americas who roamed the Atlantic shipping routes in search of their prey. But piracy is far older—and more global—than these common conceptions. Many pirates operated principally in the Mediterranean Sea, others in the Persian Gulf. Asian pirates infested the rivers of China, the South China Sea, and the East Indies. No place where valuable goods were traded and transported, in fact, could be considered safe from pirates.

Among such notorious pirates were the Barbary corsairs, organized cohorts of privateers employed by the Ottoman Empire to plunder at will or to seek revenge against the crusading Catholics of Spain and Rome who had conquered Northern Africa in the late 1400s. Beginning in the 1500s, for the next three centuries, the corsairs made it their mission to terrorize ships and coastal towns from Greece and Italy, around the Iberian peninsula, all the way to Iceland.

Operating from the ports of Tunis, Tripoli, or Salé, or the natural harbor of Algiers, the Muslim corsairs often took European slaves, whom they pressed into service aboard galleys or sold in African markets. A typical galley—a long, narrow ship suited to coastal waters—might require two hundred men to row. Christians who found themselves in such dire circumstance sometimes converted to Islam to save their lives or ransom their freedom; others became renegadoes, mercenaries legally authorized to plunder Mediterranean ships.

The European counterparts on which they preyed, of course, seldom treated their enemies any better. In 1584, the Venetians captured a galley bound for Tripoli. Every soul on board, including 50 Moors, 75 Turks, 174 renegadoes, and 45 women, was slaughtered.

The Turkish pirate Khizr or Oruj Reis, known to

the Europeans as Barbarossa for his red beard, together with his brother Aruj raided the North African coast in the early sixteenth century. When Aruj was killed by the hated Spanish in 1518, Barbarossa offered his services to the Ottoman sultan, with whose aid he was able to capture Algiers in 1529.

As *beylerbey* (leader) of the captured territory
and admiral of the fleet, Barbarossa added Tunisia to
the sultan's holdings, creating a stronghold of piracy
that would persist for centuries after his own lifetime.
Among Barbarossa's infamous escapades was the seizure
in 1504 of the Pope's own galley and its escort. Until
Barbarossa's death in 1547, European commanders tried
repeatedly but unsuccessfully to break his tyranny over
the Mediterranean.

Citizens of the coastal European city-states justly
feared the corsairs. Travel by sea was always a risk, but
pirates conducted raids on unwary towns as well. Accounts of the time describe entire families among the
gentry who were taken into captivity for ransom. Transported by sea, paraded through the streets of Algiers,
and delivered to the bey or dey (leader) in the luxurious
Casbah, they would face imprisonment in the desolate
bagnios. Young daughters might be chosen to serve in
the harem the bey, or of the Sultan in Constantinople.
Male prisoners would be manacled to benches on either
side of a seagoing galley and forced to row while under
the lash.

Fast and easy to maneuver in shallow waters,
oar-driven galleys disguised as merchant ships were
favored by corsairs. False colors would be flown to lure
an unsuspecting victim, and the renegadoes mimicked
the language of the merchant ship's crew to hail the prey
and further entice them. An unfortunate future awaited
the unwary.

The Barbary pirates were introduced to sailing
ships by the Dutch renegade Simon de Danser in the
1600s. The shebec was a large, fast ship with both sails

and oars that carried from 4 to 24 cannons and from 60 to 200 crewmen. The three-masted shebec was very maneuverable and fast and could also sail in shallow waters. Since slaves were not required to man the oars, the shebec could carry less food and water—and more men-at-arms.

Saracen corsair ships, each led by a *reis* (captain), often sailed together in convoys. Janissaries, highly trained men-at-arms, led attacks while sailors worked the ship and slaves manned the oars. In attacking a cargo ship, the corsairs fired a broadside from the upper deck while soldiers fired muskets at the victim's deck. Everyone on the ship, even including the slaves, received shares of the plunder after the bey, dey, or ruler received his share.

The notoriety of the corsairs was so great among the Italian city-states that any pirate taken at sea was immediately put to death and their ships sold or burned. The corsairs even ventured as far afield as the Adriatic Sea, Spain and Portugal, and on to Ireland and Iceland, spreading the legend far and wide. After 1581, the Barbary corsairs were no longer used in the massive naval operations of the sultan. But

the raiding and robbing of merchant ships continued well into the seventeenth and eighteenth centuries.

As late as 1784, a merchant vessel flying unfamiliar colors was captured by pirates from Morocco. The pirates had not recognized the stars and stripes of the new United States—with which it then negotiated a treaty, a cash payment of $60,000, and a formal trade relationship. The American navy soon began resisting tribute payments to other North African countries, however, ultimately waging war "on the shores of Tripoli" between 1801 and 1815, as the U.S. Marine Corps hymn memorializes.

The legacy of the corsairs was at last brought to an end by the French conquest of Algiers in 1830, and the powerful Barbary brigands would rule the Mediterranean no more.

A Barbary shebec

Pirates of the Orient

WHILE THE HISTORY OF PIRACY in the West is largely the story of opportunism during a time of discovery and growth of international trade, its history in the Orient is quite different. It is the tale, instead, of powerful bands that systematically controlled the seas, stifling exploration and commerce.

From ancient times the Malay archipelago, the island chain off the southeast Asian coast, served as a waypoint between the empires of China and India. Whichever power could protect its own trade and destroy that of its rivals in this region flourished both politically and economically. This highly calculated approach set the tone for piracy that continued in that part of the world until the time of European colonial domination in the mid-nineteenth century.

In thirteenth-century China, marooned navy

officers left behind after a failed war set up protective gangs around the river estuaries and hired locals to build fortifications. In time these gangs gained control over goods moving downriver and between ports. To combat piracy, the Ming dynasty—which at first had built its own massive navy—imposed restrictions on foreign trade. Imperial citizens were forbidden to build oceangoing ships or to leave the country. Chinese coastal dwellers were forced into piracy for their survival, in a vicious cycle of dependency. For many years, the empire remained closed to outsiders, much like its neighbor Japan to the north.

Aboard Chinese ships, the *laopan* and the *toumu* were the counterparts of the western captain and quar-

termaster, but unique among pirate crews, the toumu was almost the co-equal of the laopan. Pirate fleets of hundreds of ships were not unusual, and their crews were often multinational, consisting of Chinese and Japanese, and sometimes Malays or Filipinos.

Zheng Yi Sao, a female pirate born in Guangdong as Shi Xianggu, built a pirate empire in the early 1800s that came to include 1,800 ships and 70,000 pirates. By 1809 her Red Flag pirate fleet had amassed an armament three times the combined size of the English and Spanish at the time of the 1588 Spanish Armada. Zheng Yi Sao's confederation followed mandatory articles like to those of western pirates, spelling out the authority of the officers and the share of plunder each crew member would receive.

Because Chinese pirates exercised such tight control, intimidation alone was often sufficient to persuade a target to surrender. Under threat—a shot across the bow—the hapless vessel would strike the mainsail or heaving to. The pirates did not even need to resort to killing or maiming to overtake their prize.

Pirates roved the South China Sea, the Straits of Taiwan, and down to the Straits of Molucca. Chinese water pirates often engaged in battle with the empire's own navy and coastal defenses. Throughout most of the Ming dynasty private trade continued in secret, with pirates smuggling goods to and from Japan and Southeast Asia until legalization of commerce put an end to the black market in 1567.

In 1644 Manchu military leaders proclaimed the Qing Dynasty, and pledged to put an end to piracy. Pirates like Zheng Chenggong repeatedly raided the coasts of Fujian and Taiwan, until in 1662 the Manchus took the extreme step of evacuating the coast. The "Golden Age of Chinese

Piracy" persisted in a different form, however, continuing as brotherhoods and secret societies until the 1850s, when European nations, acting largely in their own imperialist interests, joined forces to eliminate organized piracy in the East.

Some things never change—and today one can read news accounts of piracy in the Malay islands and the South China Sea, with enormous oceangoing container ships or luxurious yachts the targets, and fast speedboats the choice vessels of the pirate attackers.

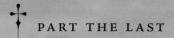

PART THE LAST

A Roster of Infamy

FAMOUS PIRATES
AND THEIR VESSELS

A Roster of History's Most Infamous Pirates

Arranged chronologically by dates of activity. Illustrations of pirates here are merely conjecture; few historical portraits exist.

BRITAIN

Hawkins, Sir Richard 1582–1622

Parker, William.........................1587–1617

Newport, Christopher....................1588–1617

Dudley, Sir Robert......................1595–1603

Middleton, David........................1601–15

Elfrith, Daniel.........................1614–37

Butler, Nathaniel 1619–39

Camock, Sussex 1628–35

Axe, Samuel 1629–45

Rous, William...........................1631–43

Bull, Dixey.............................1632

Jackson, William........................1637–45

Cromwell, Thomas........................1643–45

Whetstone, Sir Thomas 1661–67

Freeman, Captain........................1663–65

Jackman, Captain........................1663–65

Morris, John (1) 1663–72

Morgan, Sir Henry 1663–88

Morgan, Edward 1664–65

Williams, Maurice 1664–66

Bamfield, John 1665

Davis, John 1665

Hatsell, Captain........................1665

Bradley, Joseph 1665–71

Stedman, Captain 1666

Dobson, Richard 1668–71

Bran (Brand), Captain...................1668–69

Brewster, Adam 1668–69

Dempster, Edward........................1668–69

Pennant, Jeffery........................1668–69

Morris, John (2) 1668–70

Collier, Edward.........................1668–72

Aylett, Captain.........................1669

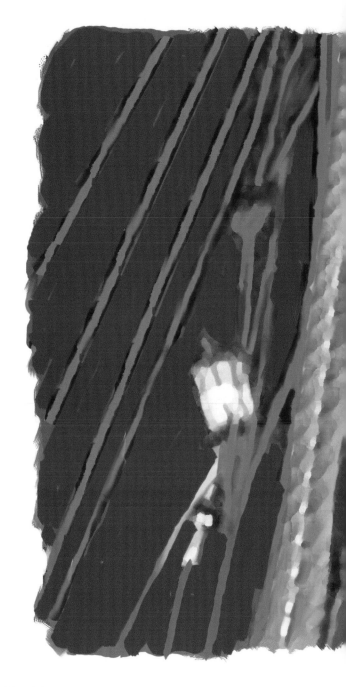

✠

Historic Pirate Ships

SHIP	CAPTAIN
Adventure	Captain Edward Teach (Blackbeard)
Adventure Galley	Captain William Kidd
Adventure Prize	Captain William Kidd
Bachelor's Delight	Captain William Dampier
Black Joke	Captain Benito de Soto
Blanco	Captain LeBour
Blessing	Captain Brown
Bravo	Captain Power
Cassandra	Captain John Taylor
Charles	Captain John Halsey
Childhood	Captain Caraccioli
Cour Valant	Captain La Vivion
Delight	Captain Francis Spriggs
Delivery	Captain George Lowther

SHIP	CAPTAIN
Desire	Captain Thomas Cavendish
Fancy	Captain Henry Every
Flying Dragon	Captain Edmund Condent
Flying Horse	Captain Rhoade
Flying King	Captain Sample
Fortune	Captain Bartholomew Roberts
Gift	Captain John Ward
Golden Hind	Captain Sir Francis Drake
Good Fortune	Captain Bartholomew Roberts
Happy Delivery	Captain George Lowther
Liberty	Captain Thomas Tew
Little Ranger	Captain Bartholomew Roberts
Loyal Fortune	Captain Edward Teach (Blackbeard)
Ranger	Captain George Lowther
Revenge	Captains Cowley, Bonnet, Gow, Phillips, Blackbeard and others
Rising Sun	Captain William Moody
Rover	Captain Bartholomew Roberts
Royal Fortune	Captain Bartholomew Roberts
Royal James	Captain Edward England
Scowerer	Captain Evans
Sea King	Captain Bartholomew Roberts
Snap Dragon	Captain Goldsmith
Soldado	Captain Dirk Chivers
Speaker	Captain John Bowen
Speedy Return	Captain John Bowen
Sudden Death	Captain Derdrake
Tiger	Captain Sir Richard Grenville
Victory	Captain Oliver LaBouche
Whydah	Captain Samuel Bellamy

✠

The End of an Era?

Today, the romantic swashbucklers of
yore exist only on the screen and in literature.
But pirates are with us still today, a deadly reality in the
realm of global shipping. Though the high-tech pirates
of the twenty-first century are of a far different breed,
and most ocean voyagers never need fear coming in con-
tact with them, the practice of piracy is still prevalent in
some corners of the earth.

Yachts in the Caribbean must still be wary lest their
craft be preyed on by drug smugglers and others who
require vessels of every type to ply their evil trades.

In some coastal areas of Africa and Asia, pirates operating from small, fast boats—better armed and outfitted than their Golden Age predecessors—have hijacked
yachts, cruise liners, or barges. The attackers have held
vessels and occupants for ransom, or seized cargoes.

Wherever world commerce advances, piracy will
not be far behind. Who knows—pirates may soon be a
reality even in outer space!